THE ATKINSON FAMILY 

IMPRINT IN HIGHER EDUCATION

The Atkinson Family Foundation has endowed this imprint to illuminate the role of higher education in contemporary society.

The publisher and the University of California Press Foundation gratefully acknowledge the generous support of the Atkinson Family Foundation Imprint in Higher Education.

THE FIRST-GEN GUIDE TO GRAD SCHOOL

THE FIRST-GEN GUIDE TO GRAD SCHOOL

Advice from One Student to Another

JOHN D. KINCAID

UNIVERSITY OF CALIFORNIA PRESS

University of California Press
Oakland, California

Library of Congress Cataloging-in-Publication Data

Names: Kincaid, John D., author
Title: The first-gen guide to grad school : advice from one student to another / John D. Kincaid.
Description: Oakland, California : University of California Press, [2026] | Includes index.
Identifiers: LCCN 2025041098 (print) | LCCN 2025041099 (ebook) | ISBN 9780520428096 cloth | ISBN 9780520428102 paperback | ISBN 9780520428119 ebook
Subjects: LCSH: First-generation graduate students—United States | First-generation college students—United States | College applications—United States | Universities and colleges—United States—Admission
Classification: LCC LB2371.4 .K57 2026 (print) | LCC LB2371.4 (ebook)
LC record available at https://lccn.loc.gov/2025041098
LC ebook record available at https://lccn.loc.gov/2025041099

Manufactured in the United States of America

GPSR Authorized Representative: Easy Access System Europe, Mustamäe tee 50, 10621 Tallinn, Estonia, gpsr.requests@easproject.com

35 34 33 32 31 30 29 28 27 26
10 9 8 7 6 5 4 3 2 1

To my children and to my wife.
You've made everything possible, and you've made everything worth it.

Contents

Acknowledgments

THIS BOOK IS A COMMUNITY EFFORT. At every step along the way, the work I've done has been a continuation of work that someone else has laid the ground for. The grad school workshops that I started in my department were based directly on the advice and wisdom given to me by my undergraduate mentor, Professor Mridula Udayagiri. She laid out my introduction to how grad school actually works and helped me shape my application package when I was sure that getting into a PhD program was a lost cause. Then, seven years later, she did the same thing with my job application letter, infusing it with energy and excitement and helping me land a job as an actual, real-life professor. Cal State Sacramento professors Manuel Barajas and Elvia Barajas offered both friendship and mentorship throughout my time as an undergraduate and graduate student. My path through graduate school was helped at every step by Professor Fred Block, who offered encouragement, motivation, and guidance through that difficult process. I owe them both so much, and the only hope I have of repaying them is to hold the door open behind me and offer the same help to as many others as I can.

My time as an undergraduate at Cal State Sacramento also introduced me to lifelong friends who have been constant role models for what it means to be dedicated to a community and to use higher education as a platform for reaching out to others. Olgalilia Ramírez, Jose Montoya, Ricky Gutiérrez Maldonado, Isabel López, Maribel Rosendo-Servin, Xico González, Andres Alvarez, Mina Naranjo, Manuel Fernando Rios, and many other extremely dedicated members of the campus M.E.Ch.A. chapter, who constantly modeled what it means to be of service to a community, and who have all gone on to careers in education, tirelessly passing on everything they've learned to the next generation.

For anyone who doesn't know, M.E.Ch.A. is a student organization that is focused on social justice issues, especially in the Chicana/o community. Working with the group as an undergraduate was an amazing and humbling experience. The people I worked with were the embodiment of what it means to *do the work*. I would sit through long meetings with people in community organizations, and when the time came to volunteer for the more thankless but necessary tasks of organizing, like making phone calls, booking rooms, or seeking donations, most people would be nearly invisible when the call went out. Not the M.E.Ch.A. members I worked with. They not only volunteered, but they did the actual work when they said they would do it, every time. I was enormously impressed by their commitment and heart, and I have strived (to varying degrees of success) to emulate what they showed me.

I also have to give special thanks to former M.E.Ch.A. cochair and current professor at Cal State Sacramento Nancy Huante-Tzintzun. She helped enormously with this book, through feedback and encouragement, and she has been an amazing friend for the past twenty years. Andres Alvarez lent his amazing talent as a photographer to take the author photo for the book, Manuel Rios lent his artistic eye, and my longtime friend Henry Pickavet was instrumental in brainstorming multiple aspects of the book's presentation.

M.E.Ch.A. also played a huge role in my personal life, since I ended up marrying one of the cochairs. I met my wife, Magali, because of M.E.Ch.A. and because of the work of community organizing. Taking the chance to ask her on a date has proven to be the single most important decision of my life. Our twenty years together have given us three amazing children—Jachel, Joaquin, and Benicio—and over those two decades we have managed to support each other through a PhD, law school, tenure, the California Bar Exam, COVID, and a thousand other challenges that life has thrown our way. I could never have asked for a better partner, role model, and all-around example of what it means to be a caring and courageous human being than my wife.

This book would not have been possible without the support of my university and my department. Cal State Stanislaus generously allowed me to write this book while on sabbatical in the fall semester of 2024, and it would not have been possible without that time. My department has been an amazing source of support and encouragement over the past ten years, from their support when I went up for tenure to their constant examples of what it means to be an engaged academic. I especially want to thank professors Ann Strahm, Dana Nakano, Vince Laus, Barbara Olave, Tamara Sniezek, Jey Strangfeld, and Meggan Jordan, each of whom provided support, mentorship, and guidance when I started this job and whose efforts created a welcoming and collaborative department culture. As Tyler Schafer, Jennifer Whitmer, Houa Vang, and Ana Ljubinkovic joined our sociology department in subsequent years, they have all kept that spirit alive. Stanislaus has also given me the chance to work with the most selfless, intelligent, humble, kind, and fearless group of students I've ever met. I've been extremely lucky to work with them over the past ten years, watching them grow, seeing them handle their triumphs with grace and their occasional failures with resolve. I couldn't ask for a better group of people to work with each day.

I also want to give special thanks to Dana Davenport, Jennifer Spencer, Emerald Nguyen, and Phyllis Jeffrey for sharing their post–grad school experiences with me and giving valuable insights into how they translated their training into jobs in the wider world. They are great friends and really fantastic resources for their communities.

I also want to give a special thank you to the team at UC Press for helping to make this book a reality. Editor Naomi Schneider took a risk with a first-time book author, and I can't thank her enough. Sam Warren, Raina Polivka, Jolene Torr, and Aline Dolinh all were extremely gracious and kind with my questions and late-night emails, and Richard Earles and Stephanie Summerhays did the enormous work of copyediting my pile of words into an actually readable book. I really appreciate all of you.

Finally, I want to thank CSU Stanislaus sociology professor Maria Mora, who has been a cohost of the grad school workshops at Stanislaus for the past four years. Her insights and perspectives have been a great source of inspiration, not only for me but for so many of the students we have worked with over the years.

I am enormously grateful to all of you.

INTRODUCTION

THE DECISION ABOUT WHETHER TO GO to grad school, what degree to pursue, and even what career might await you on the other side can be one of the most stressful parts of your college career. If you are a first-generation college student, this decision is made even harder by the fact that you have few if any people in your immediate friend and family circles who went to college, let alone graduate school. Since these social circles are often what we access the most for information and insight into the world around us, this can put first-generation college students at a huge disadvantage.

I am a first-generation college student, and I know all too well how hard it can be to find good information about what to do as you approach the end of your college career. If you don't have friends and family who can help you make these decisions, who can you go to? Where can you get the information you need and answers to the questions you have? As a college professor, for the past ten years I've been running seminars with other first-generation college students to walk them through the process that you are going through now. I've seen the struggles they encounter, the roadblocks that trip them up, and the places where they most often take a wrong turn. I've also had a chance to see how amazing, innovative, brilliant, and tough first-generation students can be when faced with adversity.

Much of the time, the issue for the students I work with is not a lack of talent or discipline, but a lack of *information*. Making decisions about your future can be enormously scary. It feels like so much is riding on these choices, and you often feel you're making them in the dark, which can make it even worse. My hope is that this book can help give you the information you need to make informed decisions about your future, come up with a plan for your grad school career, and be successful in your application process.

WHO IS THIS BOOK FOR?

This book is written largely with first-generation college students in mind. I talk more in chapter 2 about what it means to be a first-generation college student, but whether your parents went to college or not, most people can use as much information as they can get about what to do once they graduate. In that sense, I think there will be a lot of information over the course of this book that will be useful to *anyone* who is trying to plan for the next phase of their life. In some cases, you may already know some of the information I cover, but over the past ten years of working with college students, one thing I've come to realize is that no one has it all figured out, and no matter how much information and insight we have, it's always good to get other perspectives.

With that said, I should let you know that I am a professor in sociology, which is a social science. I've spent most of my education in the social sciences and the humanities, so much of the information and advice that I give comes from that perspective. I do my best over the course of this book to make the advice applicable to the broadest set of people possible, but there can be significant differences in the ways that different programs handle their graduate school applications and the process for earning a degree in a particular discipline. If you are considering a degree in the social sciences or humanities, I think that most of the advice in this book will be applicable to your process. If you are in a natural science field, or a specialty field like architecture or engineering, then you should also be getting advice and guidance from experts in those areas, who can give insights into where those programs will differ and if there are steps that may be unique to those fields that you need to be aware of. One of the biggest pieces of advice I give repeatedly in this book is the importance of building a team of mentors and supporters who can help guide you through this process, so I don't recommend that anyone use *only* this book as a guide for how to apply to graduate school or how to plan for the next part of your career. I do think that the advice given here is a very useful starting point for this process and that, if you are a first-generation college student, you will find many of your experiences covered here. Hopefully, you'll see that the problems you've run into or the questions you've had are common to many of us.

WHAT'S COVERED?

Throughout the book, we will walk through various parts of the graduate school application process, but before we can get into the nuts and bolts of an application, we need to step back and think about the bigger picture. To that end, the first three chapters take a broader perspective on thinking about being first-generation—what it means, and how to plan for what comes next. In chapter 1, I talk about my own application experiences—where I stumbled and failed, where I succeeded, and the lessons you can take away from what I did right and what I did wrong. I'm hoping there will be some experiences, both positive and negative, that you can relate to, and we'll talk about how to deal with both. In chapter 2, I go over what it means to be a first-generation college student and some of the unique challenges that come with it. I also discuss techniques, practices, and habits we can start to develop to help us deal with those challenges. Chapter 3 walks you through the process of thinking about what comes next—whether you are dead set on a particular career path or even if you have no idea what career you may want to go into, there are several steps in this chapter that will help you think through the big picture of who you are and where you want to go. Chapter 4 walks you through building a mentorship team, including whom you can go to for help and how to build and maintain relationships with people that can help you even after your time as an undergraduate or graduate student comes to an end. Chapter 5 covers the different types of degrees you could pursue in graduate school, the differences between them, and how to choose the one that might be right for you. Chapter 6 starts the process of researching the schools and programs you will be applying to and walks you through several issues that students have raised in my seminars each year, including questions about financial aid, where to get information, public schools versus private, tuition costs, and more. Chapter 7 walks you through starting your application, what to consider, and questions about things like GPA, testing, and transcripts. Chapter 8 is all about the personal statement—what it is, how it works, and how you can go about starting. Chapters 9, 10, and 11 cover the CV, writing samples, and letters of recommendation each in turn, hopefully answering lots of questions you may have along the way. Lastly, chapter 12 talks about what happens next and planning for being a graduate student.

This book is a tool to help you think about these decisions as you reach the end of your undergraduate career or as you consider returning to graduate school for an advanced degree. More importantly, this book is also a letter from one first-generation student to other first-generation students. In it you'll find advice, stories, and more than a few examples of what not to do that I had to learn from experience.

I really hope that you find something useful here to help you through the process. Being first-generation often means that we don't have the resources, the information, or the networks we need, but, with some help, there are ways to deal with all those issues and make it through to the other side. Besides, if you've made it through college as a first-generation undergraduate student, you already have practice dealing with long odds, making it work, and learning as you go. The bad news is that the journey to graduate school is going to be all of that again plus a few new challenges along the way. The good news is that you've done it before and you can do it again.

PART ONE

BEING FIRST-GENERATION AND WHY IT MATTERS

1

THE LIFE AND TIMES OF AN IMPORTANT PROFESSOR

HELLO. I AM A PROFESSOR, which means, of course, that I am important and very smart. I thoughtfully smoke a pipe in my office while I sit beside a fireplace, read thick books, and scratch out amazing insights in a leather-bound notebook. I wear tweed jackets and write fancy essays about Plato and Nietzsche and other extremely intelligent topics. Now that we've stablished that I am an expert, it's time to give you some expert advice about college, graduate school, and life. Get out a pen—you'll want to take notes.

This is a book *mostly* for first-generation college students. I am a first-generation college student. And as first-gen, it's taken me a long time in the academic world to start to understand just how much information we are missing when we start college, and exactly how much we don't know when we start to plan for what comes after graduation. Like those of a lot of first-generation students, my family was able to provide me with the big picture: Go to college, get good grades, get a job. That was the game plan, but all the details in between were hazy. I didn't have access to any source of information that could help me figure out how it was all supposed to work. That became clearer when I decided I wanted to go to graduate school. Surely, now that I was almost a college graduate, I would be able to figure out how to apply to grad school. Well, not exactly. Eight applications to PhD programs and eight rejections let me know there was something I was missing.

As much as I want to be able to say that I eventually figured it all out on my own, that just wasn't the case. The truth is that I had no idea why I didn't get in, or what I could do differently. Actually, let me revise that. I *thought* I knew why I didn't get in, but I had no idea what I could do to change it. It took some really caring and kind people to help walk me through the process of applying to graduate school, to read my essays, to talk to me about the schools I was applying to, and to write me amazing letters of recommendation. All that work by others eventually helped me break through the grad school barrier. Without them, I wouldn't have gone on to a PhD, I certainly wouldn't be a professor, and I most certainly wouldn't be thinking deep thoughts while I smoke a pipe by the fire. (Okay, I admit it: I don't really smoke a pipe, my office is the size of a closet, I don't have a fireplace, and if I ever had a fire the building's sprinkler system would drown me. I occasionally think deep thoughts, when one of my three kids isn't screaming or breaking things, but usually I forget those deep thoughts as soon as one of my kids *starts* screaming or breaking things. Oh well.)

After I received all that help, my eight rejections turned into four rejections and four acceptances over the course of one year. It seemed impossible. More than that, it seemed like a trick. My grade point average (GPA) hadn't suddenly turned into a 4.0 (more on that later), my test scores were the same, and my letters of recommendation were from almost all the same people. How could a few small changes have made the difference between being told, a year earlier, that I wouldn't be able to pursue my dream and now being invited to come study with some of the smartest people I've ever met? Instead of feeling like I'd won, I felt like I must have cheated. Or more accurately, like the system itself was cheating. College wasn't supposed to be about insider info, it was supposed to be about potential, intelligence, and hard work. But for me, the difference between acceptance and rejection was talking to the right people and making a few key changes on my application.

After I started my PhD program and eventually started to teach my own classes, I looked back at the help I had been given. If I hadn't been accepted into these programs by virtue of my own personal genius, but instead because of my use of key information, then it didn't seem fair that other people didn't have this information. I know I'm smart, but I'm not a genius. If information was the difference between getting in and being rejected, it didn't seem right not to share the same info with whoever else needed it.

This book continues my effort to pass along the information that helped me so much nearly twenty years ago. Since then, I've worked with undergraduates every semester for more than ten years. I've held workshops on personal statements, GPAs, letters of recommendation, and every other topic you can imagine in relation to graduate school. I've met a ton of other first-generation college students and had many conversations about the things that scare us, hold us back, and keep us from getting to the next level. I've also had a chance to see the unique skills and traits that we have as first-generation students, and the tools we've had to develop to survive in unknown territory. Everything in this book is based on my personal experiences and on my professional experiences working with other first-generation students. The suggestions I make here have come from seeing hundreds of students struggle in many of the same ways and trying to find effective ways to help them. But before we get into the details, let me tell you a little more about myself.

ABOUT ME

Let me start off by letting you know exactly who is about to give you college advice. My undergraduate college career consists of at least three different community colleges, failing out of San Diego State University (aka Cal State San Diego), and taking around six years to finish a bachelor's degree, with a stunning overall GPA of 3.0001. Let me tell you, I worked hard to get my GPA to that 3.0001. I'm proud of that 3.0001. At one point, my GPA was below 2.0, and it took every single A that I could scrape together over four years to get back to a B average.

I know this isn't exactly the résumé you might expect from a professor, but *I am actually a real professor!* I failed classes, I got kicked out of a state college, and, until I started taking sociology classes, my GPA was low enough to mean that I was pretty much on permanent academic probation. Despite all of this, I was able to turn things around, get some decent grades, find an academic program I was passionate about, and ride that energy all the way into a PhD program and, eventually, a job as a professor. I would love to be able to say that this 180-degree turn was due to my own intelligence, hard work, and grit, but the reality is that I had a ton of help along the way.

Once I started planning to go into a PhD program, it became obvious how little I knew about the college and graduate school process. College had always seemed straightforward: You get good grades in high school, you get into a college, you get more good grades, and eventually someone gives you a job and some money. That's how it works, right? Well, the further along I went, the more I realized that there were myriad details in between all these steps that I had no idea about. I had some vision of the big picture. But I had no idea how the different pieces connected or how exactly I was supposed to access and take advantage of these different systems in the academic world.

HOW I FAILED AND HOW YOU CAN TOO

At one point in my early education, I was a rock star. I got amazing reviews from my teachers, and they recommended I go on to advanced programs in junior high and high school. I aced tests, flew through assignments, and read every Encyclopedia Brown book I could get my hands on (I'm old, ask your parents who that is . . . or maybe your grandparents). Junior high was when I started to have some problems. Managing multiple classes and teachers was hard, I found myself distracted all the time, and trying to stay on task was getting harder and harder. I found out a lot later that I had a lot of symptoms of ADHD, but when I was a kid that was something few people knew much about, let alone looked for or helped kids out with. My parents didn't really know what to do with me.

Neither of my parents had completed college. They met while taking courses at Cal State Sacramento but dropped out to get married and have a family. For most of my childhood, my dad drove a truck to deliver furniture around Sacramento, and my mom worked in the home, raising and homeschooling my sisters and me. Like a lot of parents, they believed that a college education was an important goal and one I should have, but neither of them could really tell me much more than that. Eventually, my dad went on to earn an associate's degree from one of our local community colleges, because the air force base in town hired him to do electronics work, trained him on the job, and paid for him to go to school. A great career path if you can get it—but unfortunately you can't, because those types of jobs don't exist anymore.

My mom and dad were always proud when I got good grades, and even though I don't remember having a lot of conversations about college, I do remember getting the feeling that college was something that smart people did, and that it was something I should do. Practically speaking, what it meant for me was that I knew that I *should* go to college, but I didn't know much more than that. Where should I go to college? Who knows. What should I study when I get there? No idea. What jobs would make me happy after graduating? Anybody's guess. Was there anyone in the family I could talk to about the whole thing? Not really. I've found out over the years that this is a situation faced by many first-generation college students and other working-class students. Our families are great, they support us, but they can't give us any real information about how college works, much less an understanding of the types of jobs we might get with a particular college degree.

On a whim, the year after high school, after getting mediocre grades in junior college classes, I applied to a prestigious state school (Cal Poly) to try to be near my girlfriend. I didn't get in, but I was accepted to Cal State San Diego, which was far enough away from home to feel like really going to college. But when I got the news from the financial aid office that my family made too much for me to qualify for the full range of grants, and my parents told me they didn't think they could cosign any student loans for me, I felt like I was staring a bleak future straight in the face.

Eventually, my parents decided to cosign for the student loans, even though they were worried it would mean a hit to their credit score and possibly make it impossible for them to be homeowners in the future. It really felt heavy, like my going to college was a burden on others. That might have motivated some people, but I sort of wilted under the pressures of expectations, of feeling lost, and of being far from home with no one to talk to.

My parents could see that I was struggling but didn't know what to do. I remember one night on the phone, my mom told me that "college isn't for everyone," which I now see as her trying to reassure me that college wasn't the only path forward in life—but at the time, all I heard was that I might not be cut out to be a college student. At that point I didn't have any real evidence that she was wrong. The further I went in my education, the more my bad study habits started to catch up with me. The fact that I could usually write a paper the night before and manage to get a good grade became a problem when I had multiple projects to juggle. When I started to see that some of my grades weren't so good anymore, I didn't really have the tools I needed to build good study habits or plan projects in a way that didn't require last-minute panic as a motivator. I could do good work in the classes I enjoyed, but I couldn't bring myself to pay attention when the material wasn't something I cared about or was interested in. All the signs seemed to be pointing in the same direction, my grades were bad, I felt horrible, and when I got an F in an introductory biology class, Cal State San Diego let me know that my GPA was too low and I wouldn't be allowed back the next year.

Knowing all this, if you would rather be taught by a person who breezed through their undergrad degree and went on to be a rock-star academic at Princeton, I totally get it. But if I can make a pitch for myself, let me say this. I know what it feels like to fail. I know what it feels like to be rejected, to be told no, to be told that maybe I just wasn't cut out for college. I also know what it feels like to use all that bullshit as motivation to keep going. I know what it's like to knock on doors that seem like they will never open, and I even know what it's like to kick a few of those doors in when they won't answer. If any of this sounds like you, and you might like to kick down a few doors of your own, then this book is for you. On the other hand, if your goal in life is to be a professor in a tweed jacket with patches on the elbows and a fancy pipe you smoke by the fire while you think deep thoughts about life . . . still, buy this book. I need the money, and you sound cool.

MY APPLICATION PROCESS

The fall semester before I graduated, I started the process of trying to apply to graduate schools. I had no idea what to do or where to start. I had no idea what the differences between various schools or programs were, so I chose the schools I applied to partly on the basis of which ones had football teams I had heard of. That might sound crazy, but as a working-class kid, my biggest exposures to what college might be like were movies depicting students at Harvard or Yale and the football games I watched on Saturday mornings. Since I didn't think I would be able to get into Harvard or Yale, that left the football schools, so I applied to Notre Dame, USC, UCLA, and a few others I'd heard of at some point. I researched what I would need to do to apply and realized that I was going to need some letters of recommendation. That's when the first big blow hit. The professor I had been talking with the most up to that point was on sabbatical, and as far as I knew that meant she was off-limits. I imagined getting a disappointed email from her if I reached out, saying something like, "Don't you know that you're not allowed to talk to me this semester?"

I scrambled a bit at that point, trying to find another letter writer. I was doing well in a particular sociology class that semester, so I talked to the professor, who agreed to write me a letter of recommendation. Two weeks before the deadline, he wrote it before he left for the winter break. The problem was that he had written me *a* letter of recommendation, and I needed a total of *eight*. I left messages, I asked at the front desk, and I checked his office every day, hoping he could provide another letter, but he was nowhere to be found. That left me scrambling, with a deadline running up fast. I eventually found a person I knew who would write one, but because it was so last minute, the letter was generic. It was well-meaning and really kind, but it wasn't something that helped my application at all.

I was also in a huge bind trying to get all my transcripts together. My many years bouncing around community colleges in Sacramento and San Diego (about four hundred miles apart) meant that I had to order transcripts from Southern California to be rush processed and sent to me by overnight mail so that I could put them in my physical application package. Adding in the cost of the applications themselves, the money I paid to take the GRE (another story for another time), and the time and energy I was spending running around to make all of this happen, it all cost a fortune. Having got all that done, I barely had any time to work on my statement of purpose. Nevertheless, through some small miracles, I got out all the applications to all the schools and settled in to wait. If you don't know yet, you'll know soon that the waiting is the worst part of the whole thing. At least when you are in the middle of an application you have something to do, you have a task, something to accomplish or to work on. When you're waiting, there is nothing to do but compulsively check your email or, if you're as old as me, run out to the mailbox as soon as you hear the letter carrier come by.

After a couple months, I started to hear back. It was not great. I began to get one thin envelope after another in the mail. Even now, more than twenty years later, I still pretty much know those rejection letters by heart. "Dear XXX, thank you for applying to XXX. Unfortunately, we are unable to offer you admission for the upcoming school year. Blah blah blah, many qualified applicants, blah blah blah, wish you the best, etc." Ugh. It felt horrible. It felt like each of those schools had personally looked deep into my soul, assessed my worth as a human being, and said, "We'll pass."

As the spring semester was getting under way and I was starting to get the rejection letters, I went to visit my mentor who had been on sabbatical in the fall and was now back in her office. When I told her what was going on, she looked shocked. "Why didn't you tell me you were applying?" I wanted to scream, "Because you were on your super-private fancy college vacation, and I wasn't allowed to talk to you!" I didn't say that, but I wanted to. She looked at me like she hadn't realized, up to that point, that I was a little dumb and that she was going to need to start using smaller words around me if I was going to learn anything. She explained that I could have messaged her at any point and she would have been happy to help. Crap.

I'll skip the next six months of more thin envelopes, weird jobs, and the crappy apartment that made up my life at the time. What is important is what happened when I started working on my applications the second time around. Now that my mentor was on campus and we sat down to plan my applications, she looked at my previous material, shook her head, and basically told me I needed to start over. She walked me through picking schools according to a criterion that didn't involve who had the most famous football teams. We went step by step through my statement of purpose, my writing sample, my research agenda. Some things were kept from my first application package, some were thrown out. Instead of trying to write the perfect cover letter the night before it was due, I went through four or five drafts before we decided it was ready. The point was, I had help from someone who knew what they were doing.

The rest of the year played out much like the year before. I spent a lot of money sending my application packages through the post office. I spent a lot of time nervously waiting and watching my letterbox. But then a miracle happened. A sociology professor at UC Santa Cruz called me on my cell phone. He wanted to talk about me coming to study with them, and about my financial package. I was in shock. In the weeks that followed, I got a couple of rejections, but I also got three more acceptances.

It felt unreal, and in a weird way it felt like a trick. You see, when I had applied the first time around, I knew that my GPA was not great, that my GRE scores were okay but not outstanding, and that overall my background was probably not what PhD programs were looking for. In a way, it had made sense when I got rejected. I had been hopeful, but to be honest, I was expecting this. When I applied the second time around, not much had changed. My GPA had gone up a little bit, but only by a tiny margin. My essay and my writing sample were different, yes, but I still had pretty much the same letters from almost the same people, and I hadn't bothered to retake the GRE. Why would restructuring my essays and applying to different schools change so much about the outcomes?

If all that changed was getting the right information from the right person and making the right tweaks to my application, then getting accepted versus getting rejected felt more about knowing the right people than a judgment about my worth as a potential scholar. It felt like instead of doing something amazingly different from one year to the next, I had instead learned the secret handshake, and it had opened doors that had seemed to be locked shut. This all came with a type of crisis. It meant that getting in was less about my amazing personal accomplishments than it was about having insider information. For a working-class kid, a certain resentment can come from thinking that others are getting more opportunities than you, or are getting ahead in life, not because of what they've done or how smart they are, but because of who they know and the circles they have access to. Now it felt like I was on the other side of that equation—someone had given me a golden ticket, and I was being ushered into a place that had previously been off-limits.

At some point in your life, you'll have one of these moments too. A time when you find a loophole in a system or realize that there are opportunities that others don't know about yet, or knowledge that you have that others don't. When this happens, you always have a choice. Do you keep this info to yourself, or do you share it? As a kid from a blue-collar household, the lesson I had learned was that you don't hoard resources, you share them. Getting ahead is great, but not if it means you need to keep the secrets to your success to yourself.

This book is my way of trying to hold the door open behind me, just like my mentors did for me. Graduate school can be a ticket to better job opportunities, to more fulfilling types of work where you have more freedom of expression and creativity. It can mean more resources—not only money, but more time and less stress. Having access to all of this can literally mean that a person lives longer. This means something to me because the previous generations of men in my family have worked hard and died young. My grandfather had a heart attack at fifty, and my dad died from cancer at the same age. Better medical care, less stress, less wear and tear on their bodies might have made a difference for both. If having a master's degree or a PhD can get people access to those resources, then I intend to give as many people as possible the tools handed down to me that got me access to that world. If you're reading this, you're probably still on the other side of a locked door, trying to find a way to get through. I hope this book helps you kick that door in, and I hope that once you do, you'll hold it open for those coming after you.

HOW TO USE THIS BOOK

If you already have a good idea what kinds of programs to apply to, what your career goals are, and how a graduate degree fits in, this book offers a practical game plan. The following chapters will walk you through everything from researching schools and programs to building a support team, talking to professors, and writing application materials. If, on the other hand, you're still exploring or haven't thought through your educational and career goals, or even if you're not sure that grad school belongs in your future, this book can help with those questions, too. You'll learn how to think about a future career, how to make a plan to match your career goals with graduate degrees, and how to get the information you need to make these decisions. My hope is that no matter where you are in the process, you will find useful information. Some of the following chapters will be in step-by-step instructional format, and some will have stories and anecdotes that I hope will give you a broader understanding of the process as a whole and how to make sense of it all. Even though you may believe that the step-by-step instructions are all you need, I hope you'll take time to read through the stories and the explanations. I've learned the hard way, over my many years in education, that understanding *how* to follow steps is a very different thing than understanding *why* you are following the steps and how one part of the process relates to another. Understanding the big picture, how the pieces fit together, and why you are taking the steps you are will help you make better decisions about your future, in and out of school. While a checklist of steps can be really useful, my baseline assumption is that human beings learn best through stories and examples. Our brains process stories much more easily than lists of information, and stories provide meaning that can help us gain understanding in ways that a checklist can't. Use the guides, work through the different steps, but also read through the stories to get more insight into the process as a whole.

I'll do my best to show you how to avoid the traps I fell into, and to pass along the good advice that helped me climb out of those bad situations. Had it not been for a few caring and insightful people, I think I would have gotten lost in the cracks and never finished my education. I was extremely lucky they showed me how these systems work and gave me the right information at the right time, enabling me to get to the next level. It was never spoken, but I always felt there was an implicit understanding that I would do the same for others when able to, and that's what I've tried to do ever since. Some of the things I'll be passing along are tips and tricks from an insider, some provide a peek behind the curtain of the university, and others are rules and regulations that too often are hidden from those who need to know about them. One key message to remember is this: Don't give up. These systems were not made with all of us in mind, and in many cases they were made to keep us out. But if I've learned anything from sociology, it's that institutions, like water, will take the easiest path presented to them. If you can be persistent, if you can stand strong against the pressure to give up, at some point it will be easier for the institutions to let you in than to keep denying you access. If you know how these seemingly impenetrable systems work, you can sometimes bend the rules of the game in your favor. Be patient, be stubborn, be brave. But most of all, *don't give up.*

COMMON MISCONCEPTIONS ABOUT APPLYING TO GRAD SCHOOL

1. There is no financial aid for grad school programs.
   - Financial aid is still available for grad school, though some programs like Cal Grants and the Pell Grant are not available. Grad students are eligible for certain grants, scholarships, and subsidized student loans.
   - You fill out a FAFSA, just as you would for undergrad programs.
2. You need to have a master's degree to apply to PhD programs.
   - This is not true of most programs. A majority of PhD programs accept people with only a bachelor's degree.
   - If you are interested in a PhD, going into a master's program first may not be the best idea.
3. You need to be done with your bachelor's degree to apply for a graduate program.
   - Programs will take your application with the understanding that you will be finished with your degree by a certain date before you start their program, usually at some point in the summer. The date will vary from program to program.
4. You have to have an amazing GPA or super-high test scores to get into a graduate program.
   - GPA and test scores are important, but a lot of other factors go into programs' acceptance decisions. As long as you meet the minimum GPA requirement for a program (usually ranging from 2.5 to 3.0), you should consider applying to it.
5. You need to have a bachelor's degree in the same discipline that you are applying to study in grad school.
   - Not necessarily. While some programs will require a specific bachelor's degree, many do not. For instance, many sociology programs will accept students who have a range of bachelor's degrees. You can use your essay to make a case for why your particular background is a good fit for the program you are applying to.

- Some programs will have prerequisites—classes they want you to have taken. Check with each program you are applying to.

6. The process for applying to graduate programs is the same at every school.
   - That's not necessarily the case. You'll need to research each program carefully, because different departments can set their own due dates and can have their own requirements. Research, research, research!
7. You can apply to only one graduate program at each university.
   - You can often apply to multiple programs at a university, but the process to do so may be a little tricky. If you know that you may want to apply to multiple programs, start your research early on how to submit each application!
8. You need to be a star student for professors to write you letters of recommendation.
   - Not true! We write letters for students all the time who didn't have the absolute best grade in the class. Showing interest in going to grad school, coming to office hours, and getting to know your professors are the best ways to get letters of recommendation—not being a perfect student.
9. You don't need to bother about your applications until a few weeks before they are due.
   - Definitely not true. A lot of work and planning goes into a good grad school application, so starting early is a really good idea.
10. You need to be a genius to go to grad school, especially a PhD program.
    - Not the case. The same skills that got you through your undergraduate program are the skills you'll need to get through a grad program. If you can graduate with a bachelor's degree, you can graduate with a master's or a PhD. It's not easy, but it is absolutely achievable.

11. You get only one shot at applying.
    - You can apply to programs as many times as you want. Not getting in on one try is not necessarily a sign that you won't get in the next time. The admission committees' members change frequently, so the people who read your application one year may not be the ones who read it the next year.

2

BEING FIRST-GENERATION

THIS BOOK IS MOSTLY FOR first-generation college students, largely because I am a former first-gen college student who works with first-gen college students. There are millions of us out there, and as we gain access to more institutions, we are constantly finding that we are entering unfamiliar spaces each time we find new opportunities. This can be a huge challenge—being a trailblazer comes with a cost and with unique challenges. One of the big points I am going to make across this book is that we need to really assess both who we are and the challenges we face in order to make good decisions. In this chapter, we are going to discuss who is a first-generation college student, what it means to be first-generation on a practical level, and some of the unique challenges that come with being in this category. Not all of these definitions and experiences are going to apply only to first-generation college students—in fact, I think that many of them apply to people across the board, whether their parents graduated from college or not. But being a first-gen college student can mean facing and trying to navigate multiple challenges all at once. Let's spend some time walking through what being first-gen means, what obstacles frequently come with being a part of this group, and some things we can do to help deal with the pressure.

WHAT IS FIRST-GENERATION?

What makes a person a first-generation college student? The typical definition is someone attending college whose parents have not received a four-year college or university degree. Pretty straightforward: If your parents didn't go to college, you're first-gen. But other definitions or exceptions get thrown around. For instance, I'm the oldest child in my family, but technically, two of my sisters finished their bachelor's degrees before I did—so am I still a first-generation college student? Furthermore, my dad earned an associate's degree when I was in grade school, and eventually, after I was already in a PhD program, my mom went back to school and finished a degree in English—what about that? I've also had a lot of students who felt uncomfortable using the label "first-generation" because of some circumstance or other that didn't quite fit the official definition. There can be a lot of confusion and a little self-consciousness about labeling yourself first-generation—will someone down the line call you out and declare that you aren't really a first-generation college student?

I think the reality is that first-generation college students come from a variety of backgrounds and experiences, but the big qualifying question for me is this: *Did your parents or other members of your immediate family have information or resources that were available to you that helped you navigate your college process?* If the answer is "Not really," then for all effective purposes you are first-generation. For instance, although my dad did earn that associate's degree when I was very young, the only college advice he ever really gave me was to "hang out a lot around the financial aid office," because sometimes they had extra money and if they knew me, I might be in a good position to get it. Not the worst advice, but also not super-helpful when it came to things like picking a major, knowing how to deal with a bad grade, how to communicate with professors, and the difference between a master's degree and a PhD. Those weren't questions either of my parents could help with.

The real question here is the type of networks you had access to when you were growing up. No matter who you are and no matter the circumstances, we all had access to some networks of people and resources before we came to college. The issue is what type of assistance those networks could give us, and whether that assistance would be useful to our time in higher education. For most of my young life, my dad was a furniture mover and truck driver. My grandpa did electronics work for a local home alarm company, and the women in my family worked in offices as administrative support or handled the work of keeping the children from destroying everything in sight. All these jobs were valuable, honest labor that kept us fed and sheltered, and if it came down to it, I could have used those networks to get a manual-labor job in one of the companies that my family members worked in. In fact, in high school, my dad brought me along on a few furniture-moving jobs and I made some extra money. However, those networks fell short when I needed help with issues related to college and the types of jobs that I would potentially be doing with a college degree.

I can compare the networks and resources I had as a kid to the access my children have now: Both of their parents have advanced degrees and have held positions in several higher-paying institutions. We have family and friends who work in colleges, nonprofits, government, and the private sector. Our daughter is turning sixteen soon and is considering getting a job. She could absolutely get one at the local grocery story or pizza place, but we can also use our networks to get her an internship in an office, making connections with people who could hire her when she graduates from college later in life. Those just weren't the type of resources that either my wife or I had access to when we were kids or starting out in college, and I'm guessing it's a similar story for most of you.

Being first-generation basically means having to find for yourself all the resources that my kids have access to by default. It means having to do extensive internet searches, talk to strangers, and piece together for yourself the knowledge and insights that my kids will get just by having a conversation with a family member. The quality of information will likely be different, and the amount of work that each will have to do to get that information will be vastly different. Being first-generation means having the extra burden of trying to decipher an entirely new set of institutions all by yourself, while also having to keep up with the same schoolwork as the people around you. That can add a lot of mental and emotional stress, not to mention the fact that when we graduate, we will need to do it all over again in order to decode the world of work and careers.

There are benefits to being first-generation that come with all that extra stress and extra work. One is that by the time you graduate college, you will have had a lot of practice deciphering the institutions around you in ways that other people won't even need to consider. That's practice for the same work that you will be doing after graduation. You will already have figured out how to survive in a hostile environment, and you will be able to be the type of resource for those around you that you didn't have when you started out.

Being a first-generation graduate student is all these things and a few more. Even if you're not a first-gen college student, you may very well be a first-gen *graduate* student whose parents made it through college but may not have information to share about moving on to the next level of education. Graduate school will be much of the same work of network building, resource gathering, and institutional decoding that got you to this point.

What will be different in graduate school, hopefully, is that you'll be able to use your undergraduate experience to bring some people from your university into your networks, and use university resources to gain insights and information about what comes next. I'll be repeating this a lot in the coming chapters: Knowledge is your advantage in getting into, graduating from, and making the most of a master's degree or PhD program. Your job will be to gather as much information as possible, from as many different sources as you can find, to help you through this process. Luckily, this isn't a new task for a first-generation college student. You've done it before and you can do it again.

HAVING A CHIP ON YOUR SHOULDER

Let's talk about another aspect of being a first-generation student that can be a huge asset and a potential liability. Having a chip on your shoulder, having an ego, believing you are capable of great things even when the world seems to disagree, is not a bad thing. You wouldn't have made it through an undergraduate degree as a first-generation student if you didn't have some sense of defiance and anger toward those who told you there was something you couldn't or weren't supposed to do. However, that same sense of pride can be a problem if it keeps you from admitting when you need help, if it keeps you from reaching out to others, if it protects you by tearing others down. In some ways, your ego can be a type of shell that you wrap yourself in. It can provide invaluable protection when someone tells you that you aren't good enough or smart enough, but if it's too thick it can trap you inside and keep out people who can help.

Having a chip on your shoulder as a first-generation student is also not a great way to make decisions about your future. The desire to "show everyone" that you are good enough and smart enough can inspire you to push yourself to accomplish something great, but it isn't always the best career guide. By the time I had failed out of San Diego State University and had been taking improv acting and theater classes at a community college while working jobs I hated, I still hung onto my anger and my ego. They kept me going even when the world around me seemed to say that I should maybe just let this whole college thing go. When I ended up taking an intro-to-sociology class one year in community college, I fell in love with the exciting conversations we had in class, how current the topics were and how much they seemed to apply to my own life. I felt like I had finally found the motivation I needed for college, and my ego seized on this insight. I remember thinking, "I really like sociology, so I'll get a PhD in it, that will finally prove . . . something." Prove them all wrong? Prove I was worth something? Prove I was smart and not a college flameout? I wasn't sure at the time, and to tell you the truth I'm still not sure.

By some stroke of luck, my suddenly hatched plan to go full steam ahead and get a PhD in sociology ended up working out. I received that degree almost twelve years later. But I can tell you now, looking back, that the chip on my shoulder—my desire to "show everyone," whoever they were—didn't really lead me to making an informed choice. Yes, my plan worked, *but* I would be a bad advisor if I recommended this path to anyone else out there in a similar position.

When I made the vow to get a PhD, I had no idea what the life of a professor looked like. I had no idea if there were jobs out there or what the pay was. I had no idea if I would like working on a university campus, or what I would need to do to become a professor. I had no idea what my chances were of getting into graduate school and I had no idea if I could even afford to go. I didn't think about any of those things, though any one of them, if events had unfolded a little differently, could have derailed my entire plan and left me worse off than when I started.

In my mind, a PhD was the ultimate "fuck you" to anyone who had ever doubted me, even though, now that I think about it, my biggest doubter has always been myself. I thought that doing something that seemed so difficult, so outside of what was expected of me, would help to finally satisfy that feeling of not being enough. Surely, if I earned a PhD, I would obviously be "enough" for anyone. After all, who could ask anyone to do more than earn a PhD? It's pretty much the most school you can go to, it's the hardest degree to get. If I do this, then it must prove that I'm smart, right?

I had fantasies in my head of people underestimating me, only to find out I have a PhD. I would be able to pull it out like some ultimate one-up on anyone trying to test me. I imagined someone telling me I wasn't smart enough to understand something. I would be able to say, "Well, actually . . . I'm a professor, I think I'll figure it out." The sad reality is that, while having had a PhD for many years, I've never even been close to a scenario like that in real life. I hardly ever run into someone who tries to make me feel dumb, and the people who are assholes to me would probably still be assholes even if they knew I had a PhD. There have been plenty of times that I was in a Twitter fight, only to have someone search my profile, see I'm a professor, and instead of being intimidated, just say, "Wow, they let any moron be a professor these days!" Not the ultimate "fuck you" I thought it was going to be.

This is where a chip on your shoulder can lead you astray. If you think that the degree you are going after is going to be the thing to help you finally feel like you're good enough or smart enough, I have bad news. Getting into a PhD or master's program will feel good for a while, but ultimately what happens is that you are then exposed to a whole new world, where there are new things to strive for and new reasons to feel inadequate. I ended up deciding to go to the University of California, Davis, an awesome school for sociology, but I realized quickly that in the hierarchy of universities, UC Davis was not as prestigious as UC Berkeley, and even less outwardly impressive than Harvard, Yale, or one of the other elite private schools. In other words, I achieved a goal I thought I would probably never be able to accomplish, and my brain found a way to make me feel self-conscious and inadequate about that achievement within a few months.

There is a weird reality that I got clued into at some point a few years ago: It doesn't matter how smart you are, you can still be manipulated into believing things that are untrue, or destructive or deceptive. This is especially true if *you* are the one doing the deceiving. The smarter you are, the more convincing all those self-conscious and self-destructive thoughts are going to sound, because your inner voice is using all your own intelligence against you, convincing you that despite all evidence to the contrary, you're actually stupid or not enough. I know we're probably getting into way more of my own personal psychological issues than is comfortable for most people, but I've worked with enough self-conscious first-generation students to know that this isn't just something that I have an issue with. This type of thinking seems to be baked into the first-generation experience for a lot of us.

My point here is that if you are going after a graduate degree to help you feel like you're finally enough, you're going to be disappointed. What ends up happening is that you will continue to carry that negative self-talk with you into the next thing you pursue. It will become clear that no matter what you accomplish, it won't be enough to stop the negative thoughts, because the self-consciousness was never caused by your "lack" of accomplishments in the first place. In other words, no matter the accolades or the achievements, they won't stop the negative voices in your head, which takes an entirely different kind of work altogether.

Okay, then—how do you find "enough" and what does that even mean? The reality is that a fancy degree is not going to make you feel comfortable with yourself if you don't already feel that now. Finding a way to accept and love yourself is not the product of academic accomplishments, it's the product of soul searching, self-acceptance, therapy, and maybe some antidepressants.

Let me give you an example. My middle son is the sweetest person you could ever know in your life. He's kind, he's gentle, and he's amazingly smart. Unfortunately, he has also inherited my sense of self-doubt. Once, when my wife and I were meeting with his kindergarten teacher, he overheard the mildest of criticisms from his teacher, that he needed to work on raising his hand more, because he would get excited and shout out answers in class. I looked over to see him hiding under one of the classroom tables. After I talked with him a bit, he told me he had heard the teacher say he was stupid. She hadn't said anything like that, but because his brain is wired to produce those kinds of thoughts automatically, that's what he heard. My son has grown into an awesome, funny, and caring person, but his struggle has been this same issue of finding "enough" and finding ways to quiet the self-doubt when good grades and accolades don't solve the issue on their own. On the other hand, my youngest son manages to only ever hear the positive. He fully believes that he's an awesome person, and he's completely right! He's funny, a great friend, positive and happy, and nothing can keep him down for long. Even though he's a great student, he's never gotten the same over-the-top amazing grades as his older brother or been a candidate for advanced classes, but he's happy with himself. His self-confidence isn't rooted in his accomplishments, he just has a natural sense of self-acceptance. One time I overheard him singing off-key at the top of his voice when he thought no one was around. At one point, he paused for a second and said completely to himself, "How am I so *good* at singing?"

I bring this up because genetics can really influence our default understanding of how the world works and our place in it. If you find yourself relating more to my middle son and his struggles with self-confidence, I want you to consider that your self-doubt has little to do with a need to accomplish more or be better, but instead is rooted in something deeper that needs to be addressed on its own. Graduate school is an amazing tool to help you do a lot of things, but if you fundamentally don't like yourself now, getting a master's degree or even a PhD is not going to change that. There is another type of work you're going to need to do.

Sometimes, a healthy dose of "Fuck 'em all, I'm doing it anyway" can be an amazing kickstarter. It can give you motivation, something to conquer, something to prove. It can also lead you full speed ahead into deep water without a life jacket. When I decided to jump into pursuing a PhD with no information or even a real plan, I was basically trying to swim across the Pacific Ocean from California to Hawaii without taking swimming lessons first or even knowing which direction to swim in. Just because I ended up where I was trying to go doesn't mean that it was a good idea to set out the way I did.

You will have to figure out your own way to balance bravado and pragmatism, between being brave and being smart. One thing that helped me over the years was finding ways to get validation and affirmation from sources outside of school. My wife and family have been an amazing support system, and I knew that their love and pride didn't depend on a grade or a paper or a job. With that as a rock to stand on, I could allow myself to be vulnerable at school in ways I may not have been able to without them. Find your own rock, wherever you can, and when you do, use that safety to reach out to other people and help them in their journey. Allies will be a thousand times more useful to you than enemies. Don't forget, no one does this alone.

FEAR AND IMPOSTOR SYNDROME

Being first-generation means navigating a lot of places you don't have much information about and not being sure what to do first. Being in a space that feels uncomfortable, new, or intimidating is rough for anyone, but when you couple that with the feeling that maybe you aren't really supposed to be here in the first place, you can easily get paranoid. There is a feeling that a lot of people get in these types of situations, and it's often called "impostor syndrome." The idea is basically that when we go into new spaces, especially spaces where we feel out of place, or where the other people in the space are of higher status than ourselves, we start to feel like an impostor, that we don't belong and that others will find us and call us out. You might have felt this when you started college. When I was in high school, we had a field trip to visit the local state university in my hometown. It was mostly just a walking tour of the campus, but I immediately felt out of place, like everyone there could tell by looking at me that I didn't belong and that I wasn't college material. That's the feeling of being an impostor—everyone around you belongs in this place, but for some reason you don't, and sooner or later everyone will realize that you aren't actually smart enough or rich enough or talented enough to be in the position you're in. There is an overwhelming feeling that you're a fake, a fraud, and that eventually people are going to catch on.

Sometimes it can come up when you have to give a presentation or when you're writing about yourself in your statement of purpose. Other times it can pop up in unexpected ways. In my first year of graduate school, my very fashionable wife decided to help me dress in something other than jeans and a t-shirt. She had me try out wearing a sweater over a collared long-sleeve button-down shirt. Not exactly daring fashion, but I had never really worn anything like that, and the only place I had seen other people dressing similarly was in movies of rich kids on fancy college campuses. I felt like I was going to go play polo or go yachting, things I have never done before and had no interest in trying. I was sure that everyone around me could see that I was trying to be fancy when I was anything but, and that I obviously stood out as a wannabe rich kid—or, as my twelve-year-old son would say, a "try-hard." Of course I didn't stand out. My wife has good taste in clothes even if I absolutely do not, and she wasn't about to send her husband into the world looking like an idiot, if only because it would look bad for her. But in my head, everyone knew and everyone was judging me.

Now, hopefully you don't suffer from the same deep-seated psychological problems that I do, and your impostor syndrome doesn't extend to reasonable fashion choices. Maybe after some time in your undergraduate program this feeling faded, but it's also possible it will come back up when you move into a new position or a new program in graduate school or in a professional career. The bad news is that there is no "cure" for impostor syndrome, no pill or breathing technique or special mantra to recite that will trick your brain into getting over it. However, the more you can recognize this feeling for what it is, examine it, talk about it, and confront it, hopefully the hold it has on you will start to ease. Issues like impostor syndrome are another reason why having community is so important as you make your way through this process. Having a group of people that you can rely on for support, for a pep talk, for acceptance will be a secret weapon. Some of us are lucky enough to find this in our family, others among us have to build community ourselves, but none of us does this alone.

TALKING TO YOUR FAMILY ABOUT GRADUATE SCHOOL

I've had a version of a particular conversation many, many times in my office. "My parents were really supportive about me going to college and getting a bachelor's degree, but now that I'm considering a master's degree, they aren't sure why I would want to do that. They expected that after college I would go get a job, and now that I'm planning for grad school, they aren't convinced it's a good idea."

As a first-generation student looking to go to graduate school, the odds are good that you've had a version of this conversation with family. Given the scare stories that are all over the media about graduate school and student debt, you've probably had a version of this conversation even if you *aren't* a first-generation student. Obviously, our families mean well in this situation, and their fears about time, money, and debt are not unfounded. Graduate school comes with risks, and if your parents or other family didn't go to college, the chances are that while they may have a good idea that college was a solid bet with a material payoff at the end, they may not have enough information about graduate school to know what to expect. Thinking about it from their perspective, it's easy to see why they may have some doubts. Most likely they've heard the message for a long time that a college degree is the key to getting better jobs that pay more, and this message probably matches with their real-world experiences. Both of my parents worked a lot of jobs where their boss, or their boss's boss, had a college degree. From my parents' perspective, it followed logically that if I got a college degree, I would have a chance at those positions as well. But when we start talking about graduate school, the conversation shifts into a territory that our parents are not going to be as familiar with. If you're first-generation, it's likely that your family and social circles just don't have very many people in them that have advanced degrees. If that's the case, where are our families supposed to get information about the types of jobs and opportunities that are available for people with a master's degree or a PhD? When I was a kid, the only person with a bachelor's degree whom I saw semi-regularly was a great-aunt who had earned a degree in home economics in the 1960s. We weren't exactly surrounded by information about what to do with a bachelor's degree, let alone a master's or PhD.

If your family is at all like mine, the idea that you want to keep going to school can sound risky. You are entering an area they have very little information about, and they may have few or no resources for helping you make decisions and avoid getting in over your head. For better or for worse, it is going to be your job to talk to them about exactly what a graduate degree is, why you need one, and the opportunities that will come with it. That means more work for you, which probably doesn't come as a surprise. It means more research, and it also means that you will eventually need to form clear ideas about your goals and the big picture. If this sounds like you, you'll have some work to do for yourself before you work on getting your family on board. Once you've figured that part out, you can start to plan out how to communicate your goals to your family and inform them how graduate school fits in.

My recommendation: If you feel that your family may be resistant to your goal to get into grad school or just unsure what to think about it, consider this a sign that you need to do your own homework first. If you can present grad school to your family as part of a larger vision and a career path that you've researched and planned for, they will be much more likely to understand and support you. In chapter 3, we'll go over how to think about your career, and how a graduate degree might play into what you want to do. Once you've thought all this through for yourself, the information you've gathered can help you talk to your family about your goals and, hopefully, help them see the big picture.

MENTAL HEALTH

First, a huge disclaimer. While I'm going to talk about mental health and how you might approach the subject while you think about grad school and go through the process of applying, mental health is not my area of expertise. What I'm going to share comes strictly from my own experiences, what has really helped me, and what I have seen help others in similar positions. I don't think anything I'm going to say here is too controversial. Don't expect me to tell you the one magic pill that you can take or a set of exercises that will unlock your inner chakras and free your mind from the matrix. If I knew that stuff, I would take that pill myself and enjoy my matrix-free life with my millions of dollars. I don't have any of those things. What I do have is anxiety and depression, so I feel somewhat comfortable discussing those.

We should acknowledge up front that being a first-generation student comes with its own unique stresses and strains, which you've probably already encountered. Navigating a new institution, trying to figure out the rules, dealing with family, and managing expectations, pressure, and the fear of the unknown can all be extremely overwhelming. It's very likely that, even though you've already completed a bachelor's degree or are about to complete one, the stress hasn't gone away. In fact, in my decade-plus working with undergraduate students, I've found that the fall and spring semesters before graduation can be some of the most stressful that students experience in college life. At least when you're starting out, no one expects you to know anything—you're new, it's understood there are many things you just don't know yet. But at the end of the journey, people treat you like you've got it all figured out, as if you have a grand life plan that you are about to implement—when, in reality, you may well feel just as lost as when you started. Adding to this is the fact that if you went to college right out of high school, you've been doing school almost your entire life. You've gotten pretty good at school, you know how to pass classes, how to get good grades, how to write a decent term paper. But now that graduation is looming, you face the possibility, for the first time in your life, that there won't be any school left. After graduation, you will be doing something completely different. That step—from the security of school, into the unknown of work, a career, adulthood—is extremely scary, and even really good students suddenly find themselves unexpectedly stressed-out and anxious.

Okay, so you're stressed and anxious. What do you do about it? For better or for worse, being a first-generation student can come with a set of skills and coping mechanisms that can be extremely helpful in some situations but problematic in others. For instance, I've noticed that going into situations where we are unsure of the rules, where we don't know 100 percent what's expected of us, our strategy can often be to keep our head down, not draw attention to ourselves, and try to figure out how things are supposed to work. The last thing we want is to let others in on the fact that we are unsure of ourselves or struggling—we have enough anxiety to handle without the added fear that others are judging us. In a lot of ways, this instinct is not a terrible one. It makes us observant. We notice details that others might miss. We often are hyper-aware of some of the unwritten rules of the college experience, and this can help us avoid stumbling blocks that might trip others up. Unfortunately, this same instinct also means that we can be less likely to ask for help when we need it.

If your family was like mine, therapy and mental health were not things that were really discussed. In my family, we never had enough money to afford therapy even if we had wanted it, and besides, Jesus and prayer could fix your worries, so why not try that? Depression, anxiety, mental illness, or other related issues were just not things we discussed. My dad never told me, "Real men don't talk about their feelings or go to therapy," but in a way he didn't have to. The culture around us gave me the message well enough, from movies and TVs to books and music. I understood what was expected of me and I played my role. On top of that, being working-class often means that the people in our families work hard jobs, often manual labor, in tough conditions and for low pay. Who are we to complain about college when our parents work sixty-hour weeks and are dog tired at the end of each day?

This combination—families that don't really discuss mental health and a first-generation work ethic that says we need to grit our teeth and figure out how to do it on our own—can lead to disaster in some cases. When you couple stress from classes with stress from work, stress from family, and overall stress from the craziness of life, it can add up quickly. If you don't find some ways to deal with this overload, eventually your body will find a way to force you to relax. If it gets that far, the results are often not great. I've had multiple students end up needing to postpone their graduation because at some point in their last fall semester they had a breakdown and just couldn't find a way to finish the multiple projects they had going. Everyone has a breaking point, and even if you're convinced that you can simply clench your jaw, drink some coffee, and power through, your body may or may not decide to play along.

Take Advantage of What You Have, While You Can

You may not have ever taken advantage of it, but as an undergraduate you likely have some form of access to health care through your university, which can include mental health care. Some universities are better than others in terms of what they provide, how much it will cost, and how often you can talk to someone, but you should definitely find out what's available. You should check this out whether you feel you are having a hard time right now or not. I say that because I've read enough personal statements to know that many people are living with an incredible amount of trauma and just trying to make it from day to day. Many of you are handling that history of stress admirably, but just because that's the case *now* doesn't mean that it will be the case forever or even for the next few months. One thing about having a history of trauma is that if it goes unaddressed, the consequences can come up at unexpected times and in unexpected ways. You may be doing a good job holding it together, but the further you go in your education and in your career the higher the stakes become, and even though that time bomb is sitting silently in the corner right now, you may have no clue how much time is left on the clock.

In my own experience, I was able grit my teeth and grind through the stress all the way into graduate school. But eventually I ran into a situation where that strategy fell apart. In the span of a week, my grandfather had his hip replaced, my grandmother had a stroke, and, while life was fine on Friday, by Monday my family and I were suddenly taking care of two very sick family members and making huge medical decisions we weren't necessarily ready for. As this situation got more and more intense, my "grin and bear it" strategy started to fall apart. The stress was too much, and handling everything all at once was more than I could take. Luckily, my school had a good medical insurance program, which allowed me access to psychiatry and counseling. I can't tell you that getting this help fixed things right away, but having professionals on my side was a big reason that things didn't completely fall apart for me at school and at home. If I can stress anything to you, it's that *you deserve help.* No one should have to shoulder these burdens alone. So many of us are constantly asked to endure worry, stress, and pain. We get the message from society that our ability to endure is noble, but everyone has a limit, and no one can endure forever. You need help, you deserve help, and even though it may seem like trying to make an appointment with a doctor or counselor is another task to add to the mountain, you can't count on anyone else to prioritize your health and well-being. You have to make it a priority for yourself.

Exercise

This is one that is probably self-evident, but if you are like me, when stress starts to build up and papers and projects are coming up on deadlines, your first instinct is to devote all available time to the things that are stressing you out. That, or just checking out and avoiding the issues altogether. Neither is a great option. The reality is that, as you move forward in your graduate school career, you will constantly face deadlines and minor crises in one form or another. If the coping mechanism you've practiced most is just grinding out the work until you collapse, then that will be the most natural habit to fall back on. My suggestion is that you have to start working on new ways to handle the stress now, so that you've had some practice dealing with it in new ways when you go through the application process and as you move on to graduate school.

One habit that you can start working on now is to make time for exercise, even when you don't have time. A lot of us "have time to exercise" when we "have time." With less stress and less pressure, the idea of exercise sounds nice. But when the walls start to close in, it can be really tempting to abandon any habits not directly related to the task at hand. We all have to prioritize, and some things need to be done immediately, but abandoning the habits, like exercise, that help us deal with stress will end up hurting us in the long run. The entire application process is one long experiment in stress management, so it's a good time to start training your body to react to stress in healthy ways. And take it from someone who learned this lesson late in life: The use of substances like coffee (or others that are legal in California) to manage stress is not sustainable over the long term and can end up damaging your health. Don't forget that you are building toward a career, something long term, something to last a lifetime. You're training to run a marathon, and your coping methods will have to go the distance.

THINGS WE NEED TO TALK ABOUT BEFORE THE APPLICATION

I know that you're reading this book because you want to know how to apply to graduate school. I know that talking about being first-generation is not direct advice about where to apply, about financial aid, or about any other part of the application process. However, we need to not only name and understand the issues that come with being first-generation, but also develop some strategies for dealing with them. It's important to do this now, because the graduate school application process is extremely stressful and because the kinds of challenges you face when making the transitions from college to graduate school to a career will come up again and again as you progress. The stress and pressure of applying to graduate school will return as you transition into a career and search for a job. The uncertainty you feel now about planning your future? You will feel it all over again as you head into a new job, try to seize opportunities, or make decisions about your career path. If we can find ways to develop healthy habits in response to the pressure now, those habits will be enormously helpful in the future when we find ourselves in similar circumstances. Being first-generation doesn't stop with being an undergraduate, or even with being a graduate student. You'll likely be the first person you know to do a lot of things. Taking time to consider what it means to be a trailblazer, and how you are going to deal with it, will pay off.

In the next chapter, we'll talk about how to plan for the future, especially if your vision of the future is not all that clear. If you don't have a full career path and set of life goals mapped out, don't worry. We'll talk about how to start thinking about the future and the choices you have.

3

WHAT TO DO IF YOU DON'T KNOW WHAT TO DO

THE WHOLE PREMISE OF THIS BOOK is that you want to apply to graduate school, but you aren't quite sure what the process looks like. There is a big assumption in there: that you know *why* you want to apply to graduate school and have a goal for the degree that you will earn. In my time being a first-generation student and working with thousands of other first-generation students, it has become clear to me that a lot of us start to consider graduate school before we even know what our career goals are. Many of us hope that grad school is where we will finally figure out what it is we want to do with our lives. Unfortunately, this is not a great way to make these big decisions. We need to take some time, *before* we start our applications, to think about the degrees we are considering and the careers they can lead to.

Even though we are close to graduating from college, many of us haven't had time to really consider that question, and we may not know how to even start thinking about it. We'll start off this chapter talking about some good and bad reasons to go to grad school, and then look at ways to think about your future career possibilities and how to use those to influence your choices after you graduate.

BAD REASONS FOR GOING TO GRADUATE SCHOOL, AND SOME GOOD REASONS

Before we start talking about the application process, we need to talk a little bit about *why* you are applying to graduate school. The worst reason to go to grad school is that you are about to finish your undergraduate degree, you're a little panicked about the idea of being done with your education, you're not sure what comes next, and so going for more school seems like the next logical step. In all honesty, this isn't the worst reason in the world to be *interested* in going to grad school, but it starts to be a problem if this is the only reason you are moving on to the next level. The desire to go to grad school is not a bad one at all, but there are some issues that make the choice of what program to go into more consequential than picking your major as an undergraduate.

For starters, picking your undergraduate major, by and large, doesn't lock you into a particular career field. You don't necessarily need a prelaw degree to become a lawyer, or a bachelor's degree in psychology to go for a psychology PhD. However, when you pick a graduate program, you are getting an advanced degree in a very specific field that doesn't always translate into other careers. If you spend two years or more getting a specialized master's degree, then later discover that your true calling was in another career field—or even worse, that the degree you earned is not the credential you needed to go into the career you wanted—you'll basically have to start over in a new program. That's a considerable amount of time, energy, and resources to just set aside if you start a new chapter.

Let's think about a better scenario. You set aside some time to think about who you are and what you want. You spend time looking at career options that fit with the things you know about yourself and the kinds of circumstances and situations that make you happy. You spend some time talking to people in possible career fields, finding out as much as you can about what their day-to-day life is like. Can you see yourself spending your time that way in the future? Once you've done all this, you spend time researching the graduate programs that will get you the degree necessary to open doors in those career fields and the schools that offer those programs.

You may have noticed a pattern in the above scenario: spending time. I know exactly how precious time is, and how many first-gen students don't ever seem to have enough of it. If reading the scenario made you panic a bit because you know that the deadline for applying to a graduate program is in a few months or even a few weeks, and you don't know if you can do the things I've outlined before you apply, I want you to consider whether it might be worth not applying right away, and instead spending the time to answer these questions first. Now let's go into how to start thinking about these questions and what we can do to get answers.

THINKING ABOUT WHERE YOU WANT TO BE AND WHAT YOU WANT TO DO

When people asked me what I wanted to do after school, it was always a little panic inducing. Who knows?! They were asking me to name a job I wanted, when I hardly knew what jobs were out there to want. Picking careers, we're often left trying to piece together information from wherever we can get it. As a kid, the list of possible jobs I had in my head was limited to what I was exposed to. I thought I could be a football player, a police officer, or work in a factory somewhere. If you asked me what other people did in their jobs or even the names of the jobs they had, I wouldn't have been able to tell you. Sure, I knew that doctors and lawyers existed, that those were important jobs that people did, but how people became lawyers or doctors and the steps a person needed to take to get there? You might as well have been asking me how to get to Oz or

Hogwarts—I had no idea. Now, as a professor, I run into students all the time who are stuck in the same situation. They know they have talent, and they are proud that they are going to get a college degree, but often their potential career choices are limited exactly in the same ways mine were, to what they've been exposed to through family or through TV. Not a great way to pick a future occupation.

As a sociologist, my approach to understanding the world is first and foremost through the social systems we are surrounded by. For many of us, as first-generation college students, our social networks are full of friends and family who most likely did not go to college. That means that when trying to figure out what to do with our college degrees, we won't necessarily receive a ton of guidance from the people most accessible to us. In my family, if I had wanted a job as a truck driver, or at the local home alarm shop where my grandfather worked, I had some great networks to help me get those jobs. But when it came to information about jobs that I could access once I had a college degree, my social networks were not as useful.

You will be tempted to start this process by trying to find out the names of different jobs you might want, but this is not a great way to begin. There are a million different types of jobs in the world, and knowing the names of those jobs won't really help you to know if those jobs are a good fit for you. Instead, you have to first think about yourself. The truth is, no matter how important or interesting or high paying a particular job is, if that job is a bad fit for your personality and your skills, then you will not like going into work each day. On the flip side of that coin, if you really enjoy what you do and the environments you are in, then how much you get paid will matter a lot less. In a perfect world, we would find positions that we absolutely love and that pay a huge amount of money. In the real world, we absolutely need to have a job that pays us enough money to live a good and fulfilling life, but more money will not help you hate your job less if you dread going into work each day.

Let me give you an example. For about four years, I worked as an accounting assistant in a small company in my hometown. They paid well, the people were nice, and the work was easy for the most part. All in all, it was a good place to work. The problem was that I was miserable. I woke up each morning with a deep sense of doom and depression, knowing that I was going to go sit in front of a computer screen for eight or nine hours, do data entry or file papers, make a few phone calls, and experience existential dread the entire day. The horrible thought of spending every day under those damned fluorescent office lights—sitting in the same place for hours, not moving, trying to focus on dreary data entry until my brain leaked out of my ears—was completely depressing. No matter how much the job paid, or how nice my coworkers were, those feelings would not have gone away.

A few years after I left that job, when I was in my graduate program, a friend told me she didn't mind office work at all. She liked the stability and had no problem sitting at a desk, listening to music, doing busywork. She was totally fine with giving her job a solid eight or nine hours a day, because once that was over, in her perspective, her time was her own. If they paid her a decent salary, she could use the rest of her time doing things she was interested in and pursuing hobbies she loved, like travel and cooking. This attitude was completely mystifying to me. How could someone look at the exact same circumstances that I had "escaped" a few short years ago and think they were not so bad? To me they had felt like a prison sentence.

That conversation really opened my eyes to how differently each of us can view the same circumstances and how much our job satisfaction can depend deeply on who we are as people. In order to find a place where you fit in, you are going to have to do some work to know who you are in the first place, what types of environments you like, and what you don't like, and to honestly assess your strengths and weaknesses. If you can take some time to do this, preferably with another person who knows you well, then you can start to think productively about future careers with the goal of matching your preferences and strengths with jobs that align with who you are.

THINGS TO THINK ABOUT OTHER THAN JOB TITLES

To get around our lack of knowledge about career paths that need master's degrees or PhDs, let's start out not trying to think of job titles, but instead thinking about you and the circumstances that will make the best workplace for you. Once we know more about that, we can start trying to find areas that fit.

Environment

This is a big one: Where do you want to work? Not in terms of a company, but in terms of physical space. Does the thought of spending eight hours a day in an office building, in a cubicle or at a desk, induce claustrophobia or do you have no problem with the idea? That can be a huge factor. Where you spend your time can be as much an issue as what you spend your time doing. I've met people who really need to be outdoors during some part of their days. Other people may want the stability a larger company can provide, and being stuck inside of an office building may not bother them. Your preferences can be hard to consider unless you have had some experience working in different environments for meaningful amounts of time. It took me a year or so on the job to realize that the office environment was definitely not for me, but it took a lot less time to know that I was not cut out for retail work.

Movement

We can think of movement both at the smaller scale, in terms of direct physical space and our ability to move while we work, and in the larger sense: the ability to travel to new places as part of our job—potentially to new cities, new states, even new countries.

At the smaller scale, does the idea that most of your work will be done at a desk in front of a computer seem fine, or do you need more daily freedom of movement? At the larger level, consider whether you would really like for travel to be a part of your job. Personally, being on the taller side, travel has never been my favorite thing. Seats are too cramped, and my back starts to hurt after a long plane or car ride, so no thanks! But for my wife, who is five feet tall, being in a car or a plane is just fine. She loves to travel and the need to spend time in a car, a train, or a plane is no big deal, especially when she'll be able to spend time in a new place as part of the trip. A teacher in a classroom can have a good amount of physical movement in their job, though most of it will be inside one room if the school is K–12. A social worker may have a lot of site visits, so they may be moving all around a city, though a majority of that will be done in a car, train, or bus—and they'll have to be comfortable dropping into a range of environments. A professor can work, day or night, in a lot of different places—a coffee shop, a private office, a library—but the work they're doing, most likely, is writing or grading papers while sitting in front of a computer.

People

This is another big issue that you should think a lot about. Who you will be working with can be enormously important. That can be coworkers, but it can also be the people you are helping as a part of your job. Different populations of people will come with different issues, and it will take certain personality traits to be able to deal with each group successfully. A lot of the first-generation students I work with are interested in going into teaching. That makes sense. We may not know many jobs that require a college degree, but "teacher" is one that we have all encountered at some point. If you've made it through your college education, chances are you've had at least a few good teachers who have inspired you, so it's only natural to think about going into this field. On the other hand, there is a lot that goes into being a good teacher, beyond just being a good student. Knowing your own limitations is a great start, especially in relation to the populations you may be working with.

For instance, I have three kids, and if you asked me, I would probably tell you that I'm pretty good with kids overall, but I would never even *consider* teaching K–12. I know myself well enough to know I wouldn't have the patience or persistence to be able to teach kids under twelve. Having kids myself, I know that they drive me crazy, and the idea that I would be working with them constantly is enough to stress me out just thinking about it. I also don't really like working with younger teenagers. I like my own kids, but working with junior high and high school kids requires a type of understanding and patience that I just don't have. College age and older, though, I can work with. We understand each other. I can teach, but I don't have to do some of the hand holding and constant monitoring that comes with teaching in the other grades. College is a good fit for me.

Think about the populations of people you might be working with and ask yourself honestly if you can work with that group of people over a long period of time. I think that any of us, if we had to, could teach a class of kindergarteners for a day, or maybe even a week. But it takes a special type of person to be able to do that for years on end. The same applies to working with any other populations. When I had the accounting job, I worked directly with the CEO and CFO. I learned fast that I didn't love the corporate world and the type of language I had to speak. The communication I needed to do stressed me out.

Types of Work, Types of Help

Some of you who are reading this may be interested in going into finance, banking, or other high-powered business careers. If that's you, then more power to you, but to be honest I can't relate to your motivation. No matter the amount of money or prestige of the job title, working in these types of positions has just never been a good fit for me. I'm not making a moral judgment here, but you do need to be honest with yourself about the type of work you are going to find fulfilling. Many of the people I work with are interested in careers in which they will play a role helping other people, but what that help looks like can vary widely from one position to another. For instance, at one point in time, my wife had a position as a "policy analyst." Essentially, it was her job to stay on top of different legislation that was making its way through the California state legislature that had to do with higher education, track what the bills would do if they were passed, and try to talk to legislators about making changes or passing laws that would help students. It was an important job, and some of the legislation that she worked on had the potential to help an enormous number of people. This type of job can be really rewarding, since the work done to pass a law at the state or even local level can impact thousands of people or more. However, passing a law often involves work that is removed from the people the law would benefit. My wife took the job because she was interested in helping the students who would have been impacted by the bills she was working on, but her day-to-day work had much more to do with research, talking with legislators and staff members, and doing other office tasks, and only rarely did she come into contact with the people she had set out to help.

For some of us, that type of distance can make a job less fulfilling. You'll need to think about what gives you the most satisfaction. It could be exciting and rewarding for many of us to be part of a process that leads to new programs that impact a huge population, but for others among us it may not be as rewarding if we never get to work directly with the people we are helping.

Burnout

On the opposite end of being disconnected from the population we are helping, we may also find ourselves in positions where we are providing services directly to people. These types of jobs can be extremely rewarding, and you get to help people in a much more direct way, but they come with different challenges. Often, working directly with the public means a bigger risk of burnout. I have a friend who earned a master's degree in social work and, soon after, started a job with a nonprofit that helped homeless individuals address issues with medical care, social security, food, and housing. It was a noble job that helped a lot of people, but it was also enormously stressful. Working with any group of people comes with challenges, but the challenges of working with the homeless community were of a type that caused a lot of stress for my friend. She was having to deal daily with issues of mental health, substance abuse, and sometimes the real possibility of physical violence. After a few years, her stress levels were maxed out, and she had to leave the position. She took the job because she genuinely wanted to help the population that she was working with, and the job that she was doing made a real difference in people's lives, but the type of stress it produced just didn't match well with her ability to handle that stress over a long time.

For many of us, as first-generation students, our desire is to give back to the community, or to play the same critical role in someone's life that another person played in ours. This is an amazing motivation, but we also must be honest about what roles we are going to be performing in over the long term. I worked at a suicide hotline for a few years in my early twenties. I liked the work, and I was good at it. Unfortunately, I was probably only good at it for the first year. After that, my ability to be a good counselor was severely impacted by my growing burnout with the position. The job required a lot of patience, and it also required that we talk to a lot of people who weren't in an emergency situation, and instead just needed someone to talk to, and sometimes people were just prank calling us. After a while, the stress of all the bullshit of people calling and abusing our line wore me down, and that stress impacted my ability to be patient and accessible and ready to take calls from people who genuinely needed help.

When we are considering roles that will put us on the front lines of dealing with issues of abuse, neglect, poverty, and pain, there is a high probability of burnout. Each of us needs to take time to consider the types of stress we are good at dealing with, and the types of stress that will eventually overwhelm us, no matter how good our intentions are.

You'll need to take an honest look at yourself and think about the types of stress you are good at handling and the types of stress that you may not do well with over the long term. If you're just starting out, you may not know how you react to different types of stress yet. That's okay. You don't need to know everything right now. At the very least, you probably have a rough idea of the types of stress you really don't want to deal with daily. Whether that's a type of physical stress that you know your body can't handle (I have a bad back that makes standing for long periods tough) or other issues that may make certain types of work difficult (ADHD, for example), the key is that you need to do a self-inventory and start thinking about your body, your mental health, and what types of environments and activities really match well with who you are.

Giving Versus Taking

One of the best prompts I've heard, to help someone think about the environments they may fit into, is this: Think about what gives you energy versus what takes your energy. For example, my wife loves social gatherings. She grew up around lots of extended family and was always surrounded by loud music, moving people, and tons of energy.

Being in those environments is like being home for her. She thrives at parties, in social settings, wherever she can meet new people, mingle, talk, laugh, and socialize. For me, on the other hand, those loud parties are a special type of hell. I can survive in the loud environments, I can laugh and smile and grit my teeth, but at the end of the night, my wife will walk out of the event full of life and energy and I will be exhausted. Those social settings really recharge my wife's internal batteries, while at the same time they always seem to drain mine. We reverse roles, though, when it comes to having a quiet day at a library or finding a coffee shop in which to work or read. That kind of thing helps me relax and recharge, but the quiet and the stillness can easily make my wife feel extremely restless.

The point is this: When considering a job in which you may spend a significant amount of your life, ideally you'll look for a situation that helps recharge your batteries, and not one that will drain them constantly. We can all operate in an environment that drains our energy for a while, but being in these situations over the long term will result in chronic stress and anxiety.

What If You Don't Know the Answers?

All the questions asked above can be good starting points for thinking about careers that might fit your personality. However, if you haven't yet had enough experiences to inform your answers, what should you do? Unfortunately, experience is one thing you will need to find for yourself, but even if you're not sure what environments you will like, you may be able to identify the kinds of environments and types of stress you *won't* like pretty quickly. Having conversations with people you trust and who know you well can be a huge help here. In fact, having conversations with people who know you well is probably a good idea even if you feel like you can answer all these questions with no issues. Often, we can have a slightly rosy view of what we can endure, what types of stress we are good at dealing with, and what types of environments we can work well in. Our friends and family may not have the same illusions about us that we have and may offer insights about what are likely to be good working environments for us. If your friends' and family's opinions vary widely from how you see yourself, you may have some work to do. More likely, their personal insights based on years of knowing you will help you see yourself more clearly.

NOW WHAT?

Once you've had a chance to think about these things, you will start to have a map of the attributes that may be a good fit with a future career. This can be a great way to start a conversation with some of your advisors or with someone at the career center of your college. With this basic information, you can start thinking about positions that might suit you best.

Keep talking to people! You are going to have to put yourself out there for this step, because the best source of information about careers is people who are working in the jobs you might want. As a professor, I can give you my best guess about career fields that may interest you, based on my own experiences and those of students I've worked with in the past. But this advice, unless it's about the job of being a professor, is going to be secondhand at best. There are many, many things you may really need to know that only someone who already works in the particular field can tell you.

For instance, when new people are hired, what types of degrees do they typically have? What is the pay like, and how are the working conditions? What does a typical day on the job look like, and what do they like best and least? If they were to start again, would they choose the same career and the same degree or is there a different route they would take instead? How much debt did they carry over from their undergraduate and graduate programs, and do they have any advice on how you might be able to fund your education? Are workplaces in their field hiring right now or is the industry going through a contraction or a major shift? Are there key skills that employers are looking for that you should try to develop? All of these are things you may really want to know when you are thinking about going into a field, or even if you are already committed but want to plan for how best to get ready for the transition after completion of your program.

I just got through saying a few paragraphs ago that we first-generation students typically don't have a lot of these types of professionals in our networks. So how do you find a person to pose these questions to in the first place? There are a couple of things you can do. Start by talking to your academic advisors, professors, and others who you have access to through your university. You may not have industry professionals in your circles, but chances are that your contacts know people who are in these types of positions to whom they can refer you. The second place to look is in the career center at your college. These centers can often refer you to, and may even be putting on events where you can meet, people who have the types of jobs you're considering. In-person meetings may be the most intimidating, but you could also cold-call or cold-email people who have such jobs. When we don't have people in our networks who can help, we have to do whatever it takes to find them, and that may include contacting people we don't know, without an introduction. I know that this sounds intimidating, and I'm aware that most people will likely not take this step. However, if you can bring yourself to take it, I think you might be surprised how many people are willing to talk to you.

Consider that most people never get unsolicited messages about their job or career from strangers asking for their insight. At the very least, getting an email from you will be an interesting break from their normal routine. In addition, it may be flattering to think that they have information you need, and that you view them as a type of expert. You may find that more people than you expected are willing to meet for coffee or talk over Zoom, to go over their jobs and what they do. I know the idea of messaging a stranger is intimidating, but every part of this project will require you to be bold. The good news is that as a first-generation student, you are probably used to doing bold new things by now. One more won't kill you.

IF YOU DECIDE YOU NEED A BREAK

If you are making your way through this process and decide that a break is the best thing for you at this point, there are a couple issues to keep in mind, especially if you are considering coming back to do a graduate degree later. First, think about your time budget and your financial budget. For many of us, getting to the end of our undergraduate career meant that we had to rearrange a lot of our lives around school: Our home and work schedules are shaped around the idea that we have class each week, and our budgets are shaped by the reality of being a working student. We can't afford many luxuries, and we don't have a lot of time between work and school. In and of itself, taking a break is not bad. Ninety-nine percent of the time, people reviewing applications are not going to raise an eyebrow at a year or two passing between your bachelor's degree and your application for a graduate program. There are always many people who have been away from school for a significant amount of time but who are applying to a master's program because they want a degree to advance in their career or qualify for a new position.

The thing to consider is that when you take a break, the rest of your life and responsibilities will expand to take up the empty space left behind where school used to be. Your job will be more than happy to find new work for you to do, and your boss will be glad they no longer have to work around your school schedule. Your home life will similarly find ways to immediately take advantage of the fact that you are home more often, and new responsibilities will start to creep in. More than that, once you graduate, it will be only natural to want to take advantage of the new opportunities that being a college grad can offer, like finally moving into a better apartment or buying your first nice car.

Once these things start to happen, it can be difficult to stuff your life back into the restrictive schedule that returning to school will require. Your boss may not be willing to accommodate your school schedule after a year or two of having you available full time. Home life—with child care, chores, and all the other things that come with it—is not going to easily revert to what it was before. Most of all, the new apartment rent and the new car bills are not going to go away when you start school again, and suddenly you'll have to find a way to keep those in your budget, even with new restrictions on your work hours. Having to rearrange all these aspects of your life is not going to be easy, and while I do see people make it work all the time, it just adds a layer of stress and anxiety to a process that is already full of stress and anxiety.

So, what can you do about it? First, if you know that your break has a definite end—for instance, you are graduating this spring, but you plan to be back next year for the fall semester—you can make sure to keep this in mind when budgeting your time and money over the next few months. When you start working more and earning more money, it will be tempting to take advantage of the new spending power. But if you can keep the bigger picture in mind and plan for what your budget is going to be next year, it will help make the transition easier. Second, try to avoid anything that will require a major time commitment beyond the year that you are taking off. That may mean not getting into a long-term lease, moving out of the city, or making drastic changes to living situations. To be sure, if you need to do those things for your mental or physical health, do them—everything else comes second to that. But if you can keep as close to your original time budget and financial budget as possible, it will make the transition easier.

The other major part of this is to communicate as much as possible with those closest to you about what your goals are and what you are planning on for the coming years. Your family and your partners are going to be a major part of your support system throughout grad school, and you need to make sure that you are keeping them in the loop with your plans to return to school, so that you can work with them on setting aside any time and energy they are going to need to provide for the effort. The more people you keep in the dark about your plans, the more hurdles you are putting up that you are going to have to jump over in the future in order to start graduate school.

WHY GRAD SCHOOL IS DIFFERENT THAN UNDERGRAD

Getting through your undergraduate degree can be an enormous task. There are so many things to learn, both in and out of the classroom, and adding the stress of your last two semesters on top of everything else can lead to burnout. Some students I work with feel tired of school as a whole and just want to take a break from the monotony of classes. That's completely valid, but there are a couple of things to consider when you make your decision.

One is that graduate school is not necessarily going to be more of the same. Students often have a vision of graduate school as just a continuation of their undergraduate program—more of the same classes, same assignments, same schedules. That's not wrong per se, but it misses a lot of what is different about grad school and the classes you will be taking. Personally, I loved my major classes and was excited to take courses, especially in the upper division, but I also had to take a lot of classes outside my major that were less exciting. At some point, I realized I needed to take an astronomy class to graduate, and while the teacher was nice and the class was fine, I was not enthused at all. The class was a chore to sit through, not because of the topic, but because of me and what I was (not) interested in. I'm sure that stars are some people's thing, just as sociology is mine, and they were likely having an amazing time in the class. But for me there was very little to be excited about, which meant that forcing the material into my brain took a lot of effort.

Thankfully, graduate school is much more like the upper-division classes in your major than it is like the random classes you had to take to fulfill your lower-division requirements. Graduate classes are going to be almost exclusively within the field you chose to study and that you are really interested in. There won't usually be a grab bag of odd classes in other departments, like you needed to fill out your bachelor's degree bingo sheet. Instead, your classes will be about building up a set of skills and background knowledge that you need in the career field you are interested in. It can be a lot easier to stay motivated when there are real-world implications of the material you are covering and when the things you are learning are directly related to things you want to do in the future. Hopefully, this means that studying, concentrating, and staying engaged will not be the same struggle it may have been during your time as an undergraduate.

Another thing that is significantly different is the people you will be in classes with. No disrespect to the students going through their undergraduate programs, but in half the classes you take, no matter how interested and excited you may be, there are always others for whom this class is the random class outside of their major that they were forced to take. This class is keeping them away from their fascinating star knowledge! There are also students who are going through the motions, not sure why they are in the class to begin with and just trying to survive from hour to hour without falling asleep and snoring in the middle of class. No judgment, we've all been there. The result is that you are often in classes with students who are half engaged, uninterested or checked out, and when the professor tries to start a discussion, asks for participation, or worse, forces you to do group work, you are often left having to match your enthusiasm against another's apathy. This will be much less of an issue in your graduate courses. In grad programs, almost everyone is there because they want to be. You are all taking classes in the program that you chose and almost no one is there just to bide their time. People have goals, careers, hopes, and dreams riding on learning the material, and their commitment shows up in ways that it probably didn't in your undergraduate courses. Being in a room with other people who are as interested in the material as you are can be intimidating at first, but it can also be interesting and fun. If you're able to find ways to cooperate, rather than compete, with your fellow grad students, the classroom can be an exciting environment, with people tossing ideas and insights around in ways that you won't find in many other places. Some of the most interesting conversations I've ever had were with people I met in grad school, during our courses or afterward in small groups. Being around other people who share your enthusiasm can be an amazing experience.

Beyond that, the work that you will do will most likely be much less about memorizing a set of material than about applying that material in real-world situations. There may be classes that require memorization (in sociology that was the advanced stats courses), but these classes are almost always part of a larger project that will help make you better in the field you picked. I was never a stats-centered person, but learning how to read, decipher, and critique the statistics in academic papers made me a sharper thinker and I was able to use that knowledge to gain insights into the areas of sociology I was interested in. I haven't used a ton of stats as part of my research since I was a grad student, but I've always been glad I went through the process to learn. Broadly speaking, the work that you will be asked to do will be tied directly to the larger goals of the program you are in. You won't be learning a random set of information, you'll be learning how to be a counselor, a psychologist, a physical therapist. You'll be able to imagine needing to draw on this knowledge in a professional setting in the future, and for a lot of people that idea can be really motivating.

COMING BACK AFTER A LONG ABSENCE

For many of you, this project may be something you are taking on, not as a newly graduated college student, but as someone considering returning for a degree many years after you initially graduated. One thing I hear from people in this position is the worry that their age may work against them. While I will say that in most cases this will not be true, universities and the people who work in them are not necessarily more enlightened or less prejudiced than anyone else in the world. The same age biases that can exist in the wider world can just as easily exist in graduate programs. I'm not saying this to discourage you, but only so that you are aware. I have seen age become an issue in relation to PhD program admissions. From conversations I've heard, age can be a consideration that a committee takes up when they are trying to decide which candidates are most likely to complete their program. Because of their extended length, PhD programs often have high dropout rates, and committees will sometimes be under the impression that older students, who have more time commitments, may feel more pressure to leave early than younger students who have fewer obligations. There are things you can do to address this concern in your essays, so talk about this seriously with your advisors if you are considering a PhD. Since master's programs are typically only two years, I haven't witnessed age bias play as much of a role in those institutions, but if it exists in the world outside the university, it can and will exist inside the university as well.

I also think there are some ways in which being older than the average student can work in your favor. The fact that you have had more years of life experience can be a huge advantage. Even if the job you are working now is not directly related to the field you are interested in, there are several ways you can use your work history to showcase skills and experience that you will bring with you to the program. You can also take advantage of the fact that you will likely have professional connections that younger students will not have to people who can write letters of recommendation for you.

If you're coming back after a long absence, one requirement you'll need to plan for is letters of recommendation from academic sources. If it's been a number of years since you graduated and you haven't kept in touch with professors from your undergraduate institutions, you'll need to do some extra work to reestablish those connections or make new ones. If it has been too long to reestablish connections with past professors, consider going to talk to professors at a local institution and let them know your situation. You can also speak with advisors in the program you are applying to and see what they recommend. Chances are that they have had students in this situation in the past and can give you some good ideas. If you have enough time, you might also consider taking a class or two at a community college as a way of reestablishing yourself in the college atmosphere and connecting with professors who may be able to help. The career center at a local university or at your alma mater may also be a good place to start, and they should have some ideas on how to connect with people who can help you with letters.

NEXT STEPS

Our goal in this section is to make sure that your career goals line up with the grad program you are considering, and that you know how to proceed if you aren't sure what those career goals are. The big idea is that we want to make sure that the time we spend in grad school is an investment in a future that we've had time to think about, talk about, and plan for. Grad school can be a valuable investment in your future, but if you haven't had time to consider what that future could be or what types of careers may suit you best, you'll be gambling that the program you choose will lead you to a career where you'll be happy. In the next chapter, we will talk about how to build a team of people to help you think through the questions in this chapter and to guide you through the application process once you've decided. The connections you build here are potentially going to provide resources that you will rely on for the rest of your life, so let's talk about who you should be talking to and how to ask them to be a part of your mentorship team.

PART TWO

GETTING STARTED

4

BUILDING A MENTORSHIP TEAM

TAKING ON THE GRAD SCHOOL application process, and grad school itself, is something that no one can do alone. You probably know that you are going to need letters of recommendation, and we will talk about those in an upcoming section. But the reality is that you are going to need to rely on advisors and mentors throughout this process for more than just one letter, written one time. The people you bring in to help you with this process can potentially be allies that you talk to and lean on for a long time into the future. Throughout our lives, my wife and I have received great advice, insights, and help from people we met as part of our college career. The mentors we found have been selfless with their time, and they're a big part of how we both have gone from early circumstances of poverty to full careers that we love.

The reality is that for anyone, the circumstances we grow up in will dictate the types of resources we have access to—

including not only material resources like food, shelter, and money, but also intangible resources like knowledge and experience. As first-generation students, when we decided to go to college, we walked into uncharted territory. We can't use the maps our parents and our social groups drew of their landscapes to help us find our way. We will need people who have experience in this wild new terrain, or we risk getting lost.

I know that this is easier said than done. Talking to new people can be frightening for many of us, and we often let this fear keep us from reaching out for help. In this chapter, we will talk about ways to fight through the fear, how to reach out, the types of people you might find, and how to use these networks once you have created them.

NETWORKING

For my entire adult life, I have hated the idea of networking. I hate everything about it. Networking, to me, seems like a sleazy activity in which you try to make friends with people who can possibly do you favors in the future, and maybe you will end up doing favors for them. I've seen it as a problem for a lot of reasons, a major one being that, for most of my life, I haven't been in a position where I could do any very valuable favors for other people. This was especially true when I was a college student. If I was going to meet other people but have nothing to offer them, *networking* just seemed like a fancier word for *begging*. This view started to change when I met my wife. She and I are total opposites in a lot of ways. She loves to go out, talk to new people, stay up late and dance; I pretty much like the opposite of all those things. If you're like me, the idea of networking—which involves leaving the house in the evening, meeting new people in a strange place, and chatting with them for hours—sounds like a form of torture. For some reason I still can't understand, my wife likes it. Over the years, I've come to see that my image of networking and what my wife actually does at these events are two different things.

When we go to parties or work functions, she is quick to introduce herself to people in the room. She asks some questions about their lives and their jobs, showing interest in them as individuals, and talks about related things that she does. Sometimes she meets a person who works at a place she finds interesting or who does a job that she wants to know more about. She may ask to meet them for coffee sometime, so she can ask more questions about what they do and where they work. Sometimes a person approaches her in the same way. We've met a lot of interesting people through these connections, and some of them have become friends. None of these interactions have felt sleazy or weird. Instead, they've often been helpful. In the typical situations of life, being acquainted with someone who has knowledge about buying a home or studying abroad or running a nonprofit can be very useful, depending on what we have going on. All this counts as networking. I know that as a student it feels more intimidating because you don't have a fancy job or another position from which you feel you could offer others something of value. However, networking doesn't always have to be that type of exchange. It can also just be you in a room with other people who have information that you need, or people who've had experiences that you could learn from.

Here's another thing about networking that I didn't realize until I was older. People like to be able to help other people. Now that I'm a professor and my wife is a lawyer, we are in a position to help others, help that often takes the form of advice or an introduction to someone who has the right type of knowledge to be of assistance. Being a resource in this way is rewarding. It feels good to be able to help people, and having a type of knowledge or experience that other people can use is awesome. Now that I have knowledge that others can use, networking feels a lot more like a way to pay back all the help that was given to me when I was younger. What I didn't realize when I was an undergraduate was that all the people who were helping me didn't necessarily get to where they were by means of their own genius—they needed help too. The help they were offering me was also their way of paying back the people who had helped them.

I don't know if any of this will make the process of building a mentorship team any less stressful or awkward for you, but just know that you aren't intruding or asking us for special favors when you ask us to help you with this process. You're giving us a chance to be the expert and to give back. Now let's go over some of the ways that you can find people to help you out.

YOU NEED MORE THAN A LETTER

Most of the students I work with see interacting with professors as just a step they need to go through to get a letter of recommendation. This isn't wrong, but it's not the whole story. Yes, you need a letter of recommendation, but a lot of students go wrong in thinking that this is *all* they need. When you start to talk to professors about the grad school process, a letter of recommendation is a big part of that, but there are a lot of other things that they can help with. If you don't bring them in on the other parts of your application, you will be at a disadvantage compared to other students who do.

This is why I say you need *team members* rather than *letters and professors*. There are a lot of people who can help in this process other than your professors, and the help you need goes well beyond a letter. When it comes to letters of recommendation, you will likely need to have at least two letters from professors (we will talk more about this in later chapters), but you shouldn't limit yourself only to professors when you gather information. Remember, the idea here is that we need to build our networks and start to get access to information that we wouldn't have otherwise. That includes information about grad school, but it also includes information about the job market, about who's hiring and who's not, and a million other things. You need to know what career areas are likely to need more people in the future and which are likely to be downsizing. You'll also want information on what the jobs you are interested in are like on a day-to-day basis. Your professors will be able to answer only so many questions in this vein, because they also have a limited set of experiences to draw on. While most of us are experts in our field, that doesn't mean we're experts in what it's like to work at every place you might end up in after finishing your degree. Finding people you can talk to about these questions will be vital in helping you make informed decisions.

Professors are a good place to start in this process. Obviously, we'll be able to talk to you about the academic part, but it's also likely that we have connections to people who work in or have knowledge about the fields in which you are interested. Career centers and events on campus are another great place to start looking for sources and potential team members.

GO TO OFFICE HOURS!

You need more than professors on your team, but professors will likely play a huge role. Finding time to talk to professors will probably be a little easier than with other people, because we have hours set aside each week specifically for students to come talk to us. The problem is that most students don't come. This is understandable. Students can be intimidated by the thought of going to office hours. Professors are usually older than students, and we are in a professional position, not to mention having some forms of power in the institution we are a part of. Most of all, it can be nerve-racking because students want to make a good impression but don't always know how.

There are a couple big things you should know about office hours. The first is that you are making a good impression just by showing up. Many professors have hardly anyone come to office hours, and we may offer students extra credit just to get them to stop by. If you're coming on your own, without an incentive, it's already making an impression. The second thing to know is that you don't need to impress us. As an undergrad, you have had only a fraction of the time that we've had to be able to read the various materials, authors, and theorists we have been discussing in class. You don't need to come in and blow us away with your new and insightful analysis of theory or methods. Your goal in coming to office hours is not to demonstrate to us that you are worthy of our time and attention—you get that automatically by being our students. Instead, office hours are a way for us to get to know each other, to clear up any misunderstandings or questions from class, to talk about your goals and plans, to strategize, to have a conversation, to basically just be human.

If you begin going to office hours knowing that you are planning for graduate school and that you may later ask this professor for a letter of recommendation, it can potentially add a layer of stress to the situation. That makes sense: In the larger social world, it can be considered rude or insensitive to interact with a person only when you need something from them. I remember thinking that professors would be mad at me if they found out I had been coming to office hours with the expectation of a letter in the future. I was half expecting them to say, "You've been using me this entire time?!" Being on the other side of the desk now, let me tell you that it isn't like that at all. Working with you on your questions and issues from class, planning for your future, and writing you letters of recommendation are all part of our job description as professors. For the most part, professors do not see these things as favors that they are doing for you as a friend; rather, we see helping you as a professional courtesy, something that comes with the job we have.

Even after I've said all that, I know you'll probably still feel nervous when you go to talk to a professor. It's natural, but having a plan about what to talk about can help. One possibility is to just start with the project that you have going on right now: going to grad school. Ask them what their graduate experience was like and how they chose the program that they went to. Or just look at the list of topics to talk about in office hours and pick one of those if you need something to get you going.

Office hours can be intimidating, but they are also the best way to build relationships with potential mentors and guides, people you are going to need in your corner over the course of your grad school education. Remember, as a first-generation college student, one of your most important jobs is to build the networks that are going to help you take advantage of your college degree. Office hours are a great place to start doing that.

TYPES OF MENTORS

Working with mentors can be a really rewarding experience in a variety of cases, but it can help a lot if your mentor's style is a good match to what you need as a student. Having a good match will mean better communication, a smoother working relationship, and overall better outcomes. If you can spend some time beforehand thinking through what your own working style is, you will have a better idea what kind of help will benefit you the most. This is another point in the process where knowing yourself will be a huge help. You need to be honest about the type of conditions you normally work in and whether those conditions will be beneficial for you in the long run. As an undergraduate, I was constantly waiting until the last minute to turn things in. It was a bad habit, and it has come back to bite me at several points later in life. Thinking back, it might have been a good idea to let the people on my team know this and get their insight into how I might better structure the work I needed to do so that I could try to minimize the stress I was putting on myself.

The following are a few different types of mentors I've encountered over the years. Most of these are intentionally exaggerated, but I do think you'll find some versions of these styles when you look for mentors of your own. I'm not looking to pass judgment on any one style or another, but I am asking you to think about what sort of mentorship might best fit how you work and be best for you moving forward.

The Helicopter Parent

This type of mentor is extremely detail oriented and will want to oversee your project at a granular level. They will probably be in frequent contact, demand frequent updates, and want to be involved in every aspect of your project. This mentor will work best if you are a detail-oriented person yourself and the frequent check-ins and updates will help you keep your project focused. If you struggle with getting lost in a project, the frequent meetings and firm deadlines will potentially help keep you on track. If you are not a self-starter and could use some supervision, this mentor will help make sure that you are sticking to the task at hand. This mentor is also a good choice if you would benefit from having an extremely detailed map of the project and the timeline you will need to meet to finish it. For some people, this level of detail will help ease anxiety because they have a plan to stick to. On the other hand, this mentor is not a good fit if you need more space to explore and develop projects on your own or if having firm deadlines and frequent check-ins will cause anxiety rather than help lessen it.

The Big-Picture Supervisor

This type of mentor is less hands-on than the helicopter parent. They're more about helping you see the big picture and making sure you are working toward your goal. Compared to the other mentor types, the big-picture supervisor is far less detail oriented, so you should expect to fill in some of the gaps on your own. Basically, be prepared: This mentor will do very little hand holding, and you will need to do things like set meeting times, plan an agenda for what you want to talk about, and come in with questions on things you need help with. For some people, having a person who trusts them to handle the smaller things while giving them help with the big-picture direction of the project can be like a breath of fresh air. Having more freedom to explore the options without sticking to a meticulous step-by-step plan just fits some people's personalities. This mentorship type can also be useful if you have significant life obligations outside of school, like family or work, and you know that you will need to plan around those commitments. This mentor will be a bad fit, though, if you tend to get lost in too much free time. You'll need to be a self-starter with a good ability to keep yourself on task or you may find yourself behind schedule.

The Easily Distracted Ally

One thing you need to realize is that just because we academics have finished a PhD, it doesn't mean that we have mastered the art of project management for ourselves or for other people. A dissertation is a big undertaking, but many of us get through it by the skin of our teeth, surviving the process rather than mastering it. That doesn't mean that this type of person can't make a good mentor—it's just that you need to be realistic about which aspects of the task at hand each individual on your team is going to be good at. I've worked with several professors who have made being easily distracted into an entire career. In many cases, they have mastered the art of finding new and interesting projects, taking them on, and finding a way to finish them, or abandon them when something more interesting comes along. On the plus side, this can make someone an eclectic thinker with a broad range of experiences and ideas that span multiple topics or fields. On the minus end, it can mean that staying focused on one aspect of your project may not be their strong suit. This type of mentor would be a great fit to help you brainstorm ideas, workshop pieces of your project, or help you find inspiration when you need to go in a new direction or are unsure what to do next. Having this person as your main project manager or counting on them to give you strict deadlines and clear goals may be a mistake. This type of mentor is more likely to suddenly bring up new ideas they are interested in than to stay on topic over the course of months or years. Bring this person on to have amazing conversations that might bring up really interesting ideas, but plan on needing to keep yourself focused, or perhaps have an additional mentor who can help keep you on track.

The Well-Intentioned Ghost

Look, as professors we have a lot going on, just like you do. We probably have families, work pressures, and other stressors—on top of the fact that we are just plain older than you and we get tired a lot easier. In a lot of cases, a person who has dealt with such stresses over a long period of time can be completely willing to help, and even excited to be on your team—but when it comes down to it, they may not have the time or the mental capacity to do the work that's needed to help you. Many professors in this situation may not even realize they are in it. It can be hard for anyone, professors included, to realize they're overwhelmed, and if a person we like asks for help, we really want to say yes. Know that just because someone says yes, it doesn't mean that their intention to help will result in their helping in all the ways you need.

If someone is frequently taking a long time to respond to emails, like ten days or more, or is hard to reach in their office, this might be an early warning sign that they will not have time to take this mentorship on. Even if they say they are on board, if you can't get hold of them when you need to it's a big deal. There are deadlines on this project, and missing them is not an option, so you need people who are going to be good communicators. If you start to realize that you have someone on your team who is overwhelmed and not responding, you need to start recruiting a new team member right away. Your ghost mentor professor may turn a new leaf and suddenly be responding to every message ten minutes after you write it, but for now you can't count on that happening and you need to find another person to bring on board.

QUESTIONS TO ASK YOUR TEAM MEMBERS

1. What was your grad school experience like?
2. How did you choose your major and your school?
3. What were some of the hardest things about grad school, and how did you deal with them?
4. What were some of the best things about being a grad student?
5. How did you support yourself while you were in grad school?
6. If you could do it again, what are some things you would do differently?
7. Looking back, would you choose the same program or go in a different direction? Why?
8. Was the job you have now always your goal? How did you find the position you are in now?
9. Have you worked with students with interests like mine in the past? What did they choose to do, or what programs did they go into?
10. Are there programs or degrees that you would recommend staying away from? Why?
11. What are the best parts of the job you have now? What would you change?
12. Are there other programs or degrees that you think I should consider?
13. How did you choose your mentors? Did you ever have to change mentors or let one go? How did you handle that?
14. What should I look for in a mentor?
15. Are there things I should do as an undergraduate that might make me more competitive or more prepared for the programs I'm interested in?
16. What are the major drawbacks of the field I'm interested in? Major benefits?
17. What do you think about the timeline I've put together? Anything to add or remove?
18. What information do you need from me to write a letter of recommendation?

BAD FIT

At one point or another, everyone will most likely deal with a team member who just doesn't work out in this role. It can happen for all kinds of reasons: communication differences, different ideas of how a project should go, schedules not matching up. When it does happen, how should you handle it and what should you do next? Given that there is often a power imbalance between you and the people on your team, it can be intimidating to consider telling someone that you don't want to work with them anymore. In a lot of instances, students will either avoid the issue altogether or just continue trying to make an uneasy situation work.

When I started graduate school, there was a particular professor whom I thought I was going to work well with. I took some classes from him, and he was tough, challenging, and scary smart. We got along in class, so I would bring him ideas I had about my dissertation research as I went through the program. The issue was that every time I brought him a new idea or a revised one, he would find a problem with it. I felt I could never get it right, and no matter how much I worked on my ideas, he would keep saying, "I don't really see the question here." I know that doesn't sound horrifying, but in sociology PhD speak it's basically saying, "Good try kid, but that's not going to work." After a semester or two of this, I went to my major advisor and talked to him about my ideas. In contrast to the first professor, he was immediately positive. He liked my ideas, and while he had suggestions and input, he was absolutely *not* saying that I needed to start all over or that he "didn't see the question." I still remember the meeting where my advisor told me that my ideas would make a solid dissertation. I was floored. I felt completely relieved that I was actually making progress, but also confused as to why the two professors' reactions to the same material were so different. Looking back, I think I should have gotten the message sooner that the professor I was trying to work with just wasn't a good fit. He had many positive qualities, but, for whatever reason, our personalities and ways of viewing the world just didn't match. If I had trusted myself and been willing to move on sooner, I could have saved a lot of time and disappointment.

Telling someone who is helping you that you no longer want their help is a strange situation for anyone to be in. There's the possibility of hurt feelings or misunderstandings, and most people, no matter their age or circumstances, have strong incentives not to have this type of conversation. There really isn't an easy answer. Hurt feelings can happen, of course, but on the other hand you need and deserve team members you communicate well with and who you feel are on the same page as you in terms of your application materials, the programs you are applying to, and your overall goals for your future. If you have a team member who isn't working well in this regard, no matter the reason, you need to find a way to bring in a new person.

One huge reason that mentor relationships don't work out is different expectations about time, energy, and detail. In some cases, we may be looking for a super-hands-on mentor who will go through our material line by line and help us edit and rewrite. If we start to realize that a team member is committed only to writing one letter, one time, the relationship can get tricky. If we need and expect more time, energy, and attention to detail than they are willing to provide, issues can arise quickly.

COMMUNICATE, COMMUNICATE, COMMUNICATE

The key to avoiding this awkward circumstance in the first place is communication, and it starts with you communicating with yourself. You must be clear in your own mind about the type of help you want, the type of mentorship style you work best with, and what you want out of a mentor relationship. If you can identify those things for yourself first, you will be able to communicate them more clearly to a professor or other potential team member. If they know up front what your expectations are, the chances are better that they will be able to give you what you need or, at the very least, let you know that what you need may not match well with what they can provide.

For example, I am a horrible project manager. If you need someone who is going to be detail oriented and who can help you develop a rigid timeline and then stick to it, I am not the right person to work with, at least not as your major advisor. There are many things I feel I can do well, but enforcing time discipline on other people is not one of them. I can barely keep myself on task, let alone another person. Over the years, I've had people ask me to be their thesis supervisor for one program or another or ask to do an independent study with me as a project lead. I've learned the hard way that I need to let them know up front what I'm good at and what I'm not. It can be a little uncomfortable if the student thinks I'm trying to find a creative way to say no to their request, but on the basis of my experience, I know that I must let them know right away what I can offer and what I can't.

LETTING SOMEONE GO

So, you've made the tough decision to remove a member of your team. The idea of telling them you no longer need their help can be really intimidating, but you have options. The first option in one I don't recommend, but if you have a member who is not returning emails with any frequency or urgency, and is generally hard to get hold of, you can just stop contacting them. For a lot of you, I know this will sound like the best option, since it presents the least amount of potential conflict, but let me argue that it's better to talk to them even if it's harder. More likely than not, your team member knows they are behind on getting back to you and have it in the back of their head that they still owe you an email or a letter or a meeting. Sending them a note to let them know you are moving in a new direction lets them off the hook and means they can let go of this mental block. Telling them also relieves your own stress of waiting for them to eventually contact you, ask you what they need to do, apologize for being out of touch, or simply ask where to send the letter they just finished writing for you. At that point, if you've moved on without saying anything, you have a bigger dilemma: Either respond and tell them you got other help, or ignore them for the rest of your life.

Instead, try the best you can to be direct. You don't have to give them a rundown of the things they've done wrong or why you need a new team member. You can just let them know that another person has agreed to write you a letter of recommendation and to work with you on your application. Thank them for the time they put in and let them know you will keep in touch. It doesn't have to be dramatic, and it will feel *a lot* better than just letting it fester.

This gets a little more complicated if the person you need to move on from is still trying to be an active member of your team or if you are currently taking a class from them. If that is the case, you probably need to have this conversation in person. The last thing you need is awkwardness between you and someone you see regularly. You can let them know you started working with someone else who became available unexpectedly and that you are going to have them write a letter. Be vague if you need to, but be direct if you can. It's always better in the long run for people to know where they stand.

BAD FIT OR BAD INTENTIONS?

Not that long ago, college was a lot different. The professor I had as my grad school mentor was in his late sixties, and when he was an undergraduate a call from the right professor to a friend at another college might be enough to get a person into a program. I've even heard of people getting jobs this way in decades past. Higher education was a lot more of an "old boys' club" back then, a men's organization run from backrooms, where meeting the right people and shaking the right hands could open a lot of doors for the right class of people.

In a situation like that, it was probably easy for professors to let the power they had go to their heads. If you are the one thing standing between a person and a PhD, professorship, or grant, people are probably going to kiss your ass like crazy. The attitude in the earlier era was that a student needed to earn a professor's respect and that things like letters of recommendation were privileges to be granted only to the most talented students or those the professor felt had the most potential.

Thankfully, that system is just not around much anymore, at least not in the circles I work in. I'm not famous, I don't have rich and powerful friends, and a phone call from me might not even get you a job at McDonald's—it definitely will not get you into Harvard. As higher education has expanded, no longer restricted to the children of the rich and well connected, a lot of the practices that made the old system work have been abandoned, which is good, because they sucked and were unfair. However, you may still run into professors who have the old attitude, as if it is their job to decide who has the right stuff and who doesn't, and that a letter from them is a favor to be earned. Run away from anyone who comes across like that. There are a million other professors out there, and unless the one you are working with has a last name like Obama, chances are they can't do anything special for you in the academic world that someone else couldn't do without making you feel terrible.

When students work with professors, there is an inherent power imbalance at play that is tricky to navigate. We don't have a lot of power, but we do have some power. We can grade you when you are in our classes, and afterward we can give you a good recommendation or not give you one at all. In most cases, we are older and more established in our careers and have more economic resources than the students we work with. All these differences can make interactions tricky, so if you run into a person who seems to be taking advantage of the power imbalance instead of trying to lessen it, you need to find a different person ASAP.

If anyone takes it further than that, using their position to harass you, try to coerce you, or in any way make you feel strange or uncomfortable about your interactions, tell another team member right away. Bringing someone else on board who can even-out the power imbalance is essential, and another professor whom you trust can help you find resources to protect yourself, and help keep other students from being victims in the future.

If you are dealing with someone who seems to be acting on bad intentions and is making you feel uncomfortable, you don't owe them anything. End the relationship as soon as possible. If you need to send them a message, do that, but give them as little information as possible, just stating that you decided to go in a different direction and that you thank them for their time. Be sure to talk to another person on your team about what you're doing, and save any communication between the two of you. You need to be safe before anything else.

STAYING IN TOUCH AFTER A BREAK OR AFTER YOU GRADUATE

This seems to trip people up all the time. Once students graduate, they often feel as if their access to the university and all the people there is cut off. This can cause problems when you start to think about applying for graduate school and it's been some time since you've been in touch with the professors and other people that you built relationships with over your undergraduate years. It can feel awkward or even intrusive to reach out after years of not being in contact to suddenly say, "Hey! I know I haven't talked to you in forever, but now I need your help, so here I am!"

From the other side of the desk, let me tell you that it is never as strange or awkward for us as it will seem for you. Hardly any of our students keep in touch after they graduate, so if you reach out to let us know how you're doing, it's usually a nice surprise and not an intrusion. In almost every case, your old professors will be happy to help you with this next part of your life.

If it has been a while since you last talked, you may want to remind them what classes you had with them in what years. Remembering names after a few years can be tricky, so if there was something particular about the class you took or an interaction you had with them then, now is a good time to include it. If possible, try to make a meeting in person or over Zoom. I know that names are hard for me to remember, but I don't forget faces nearly as easily, and seeing you will often jog my memory much more quickly. In both instances, communication is the key to a good relationship with people on your team.

AGAIN: COMMUNICATION IS KEY!

As you make your way through the course of this application process and beyond, communication is going to be a big part of keeping your team members on board. Every semester, I see students make the mistake of communicating with a professor once and then dropping off the face of the earth for two months, until a deadline is coming up or until the student works up the courage to make contact again. A mentor relationship is like a friendship: It needs communication and attention to grow and to give the best results. One thing you can do to help is to schedule out contacts that you will have with your team members through the course of the application process. Plan to contact each team member around once every two weeks and try to make every other meeting an in-person meeting. This will sound like a lot at first, but this project requires a lot of work, so hopefully there will be new things to fill them in on each time you meet. You can bring up anything that you've found during your research, new questions you've thought of, or new material that gives them insight into who you are.

The more you plan out these communications in your calendar rather than waiting for inspiration to strike, the more likely you will be to stay in touch.

Thus far in the process, we've talked about thinking through your career and school plans and finding the right people who can help. Next we start moving into the nuts and bolts of the application process itself, from knowing the difference between types of graduate degrees to researching schools and programs, through making a plan for the work you need to do.

5

WHAT ARE THE DIFFERENT DEGREES AND WHAT DO THEY MEAN?

ONE OF THE REASONS why I put on workshops each year, and why I'm writing this book, is that so many of us don't have some of the basic information about graduate school. That includes things like differences between a PhD and a master's degree, the realities of financial aid, and how grad school schedules work. In this chapter, we'll go over a lot of those basic questions and some of the other common questions that come up in every workshop.

DIFFERENCES BETWEEN THE PhD, THE MASTER'S DEGREE, AND CREDENTIALS

When you are first considering grad school, trying to understand the differences between the various types of degree you could pursue and the pathways to graduation for each can be extremely confusing. In this section, I want to cover some of the differences between the major degrees and go over questions and misunderstandings that students typically have about the different programs.

I want to state up front that you do *not* need to get a master's degree first if you want to go on to a PhD program. Most PhD programs accept students who have only a bachelor's degree, meaning that you can apply to the program directly without having to obtain some other graduate degree first. I've talked to so many students who had no idea that this was the case, and I was one of those people when I was an undergraduate. It makes perfects sense that a master's degree would be a step on the road toward a PhD, just like getting a bachelor's is a prerequisite for going to graduate school. But not knowing how the programs work can cost you a lot of time and frustration—and, even worse, may mean that you come to realize you've spent time in a program when you didn't need to. Instead of thinking of master's and PhD degrees as being steps on a ladder, it is helpful to think of them as separate paths that you might go down, with different outcomes at the end of each path. If you go down the master's degree path and decide later that you want to pursue a PhD, you may be surprised to learn that your master's degree hasn't necessarily brought you closer to acceptance into a PhD program, and that in many ways you are going to be starting over.

A Confusing Sidenote About the PhD

I know I just spent the last section talking about how a master's degree is not necessarily a step toward a PhD. This is true, but you should know that many PhD programs will allow you to obtain a master's degree along the way *toward* a PhD. This isn't true for all programs, but it is pretty common in the humanities and social sciences. One way to think about the difference is that many schools will offer what is called a "terminal master's degree," which basically means that the master's degree is the highest degree that the school offers in that program. If you go into a program with a terminal master's degree hoping that it will lead into a PhD, you may be disappointed to learn that you will likely be asked to start from the beginning if you enter a PhD program. I know this is confusing, so the best thing to do will be to talk to advisors and professors about the particular career field you are interested in, and they can help fill you in on the path to a degree.

WHICH DEGREE TO CHOOSE?

A useful way to think about what program you should pick is to ask, "What is the minimum amount of school I need in order to be qualified for the job I want and to be competitive for a career in that field?" If the minimum is a bachelor's degree, I think it makes a lot of sense to consider whether the time and energy you would spend in a graduate program might be better spent getting direct experience in a job. But if the career you want requires an advanced degree, you should aim to have the best match between the degree you earn and the career you want to have. For instance, if you want to be a social worker, doing fieldwork and connecting directly with people through government or nonprofit programs, a master's degree in social work is probably the best fit. For most of the private- and state-sector jobs in the social work field, this will be the minimum requirement for being hired and for advancing in the available positions. There are also programs that offer a PhD in social work, so why not go for that degree? Good question. For the most part, having a PhD in social work is not going to get you a huge leg up over others who have a master's degree, in the positions and settings that we're talking about. In fact, using the time you would have spent getting a PhD to instead gain experience in the field might help you advance more quickly or get you into the jobs you want faster than a PhD would. This is because, for the most part, a PhD in social work is focused on conducting research and publishing academic papers on the topics that social work addresses. In other words, getting a PhD in social work helps prepare you more to be a professor of social work than to be a social worker.

PhD programs often take much longer than master's programs. While most master's programs are set up to be completed in two years, many PhD programs can stretch out for five, six, seven years or even more. A master's program will train you in many of the aspects of doing research or practicing in a field and ask you to demonstrate some level of competence in that work. A PhD program will ask you not only to master those same research skills, but also to put together a research program and produce new research on a topic, often by gathering and analyzing original data. The data-gathering process alone can sometimes take years to complete, depending on your field and the methods you choose, and writing up your findings can take just as long. While a typical master's thesis is around forty to eighty pages, a PhD dissertation can be hundreds of pages. One way to think about it is that writing a master's thesis is closer to writing an extended research essay. It may take a long time and require a lot of work, but overall, the process is probably measured in months. On the other hand, the process of writing a dissertation is more like that of writing a book, such as a novel. Consider how much time you would need to produce a long novel—the research, writing, and revisions could easily take years. A PhD works on the same sort of timeline.

So why choose a PhD? The simple answer is that you have a career goal, and a PhD is the degree you will need to get your foot in the door. For many people, that goal is being an academic or a high-level researcher in a particular field. To be hired as a professor in a tenure-track position, you will almost always need a PhD. There are many research positions in science-related fields for which a PhD is a requirement. If any such positions are on your radar, you need to put a PhD program on your research list.

I bring all this up because every year, several people tell me they are planning to go into a master's program and that if they like it, they will go on to apply to a PhD program. It makes sense that you might want to test the waters first when you aren't sure what the process will be like or if you will even *want* to commit to something that will take multiple years to finish. I worry, though, that students who go into a master's program with this idea may find going for a PhD even harder when they realize that the timeline hasn't been made any shorter by virtue of their master's program.

Now that we've talked a little bit about the differences, let's explore a little more about the types of jobs that are available to those with the different types of degree.

CAREER POSSIBILITIES FOR EACH DEGREE

PhD Jobs

A PhD is a highly specialized degree that can be excellent at opening very specific doors in the employment world. In the academic world, a PhD is often the minimum requirement to be considered for a job as a full-time or tenure-track professor. The types of jobs available to a person after they earn a PhD can vary broadly, based on the discipline. For example, a person with a PhD in psychology may go into private practice, seeing patients and working directly with clients. They may also choose to be an academic and become a professor of psychology at a university. Or they may choose to focus on clinical research in a lab or an organization that needs their expertise. This would be different for a person with a degree in sociology. Since sociology doesn't have a clinical side to it, working directly with patients wouldn't be an option, but working as a professor or as a researcher could be. The most important thing to do will be to talk to people in the fields you are interested in and find out what the possibilities are with the relevant degrees. Often, there will be options you've never heard of (and some that aren't directly linked to your PhD program) that you are in fact well prepared for, given the training you've received.

Master's Degree Jobs

A master's degree can be extremely useful in opening doors to a lot of different workplaces. With some degrees, such as a master's in social work, the field you are entering can be extremely diverse, and you may be qualified for numerous different positions in various settings, from state or federal jobs to private hospital positions to full-time remote work for a nonprofit. For those with other master's degrees, such as marriage and family therapy or physical therapy, the career field will be somewhat narrower in terms of the range of jobs they will be directly qualified for when they graduate. Always be sure that the degree you are earning is a good match for the job or the type of job you really want to have, though the two don't always have to be directly related or named the same thing, the way a counseling degree leads to being a counselor. Think too about the types of skills the degree will be training you in and how those skill sets relate to other career fields that aren't directly linked to your program. For instance, someone with a sociology master's degree doesn't really have a job field called "sociology" to go into, but they will have had advanced training in research methods, statistics, data analysis, project management, and several other skills that would make them excellent candidates for a lot of different jobs. Just as with the PhD, communication is the key: Have conversations with people who have the master's degree you are interested in or who are working in the field you want to go into, and find out what path they took to get where they are. Firsthand conversations are the best source of real-world information about work, degrees, and life after education. Start talking to people now, and never stop.

Credential Programs

Credential programs are specialized programs that offer a credential needed to enter a particular field, such as teaching. Credential programs can be extremely helpful for getting into a specific field you have chosen, but in many cases they are highly specialized and may not have a lot of carryover into other fields if you decide you want to move into a new area. Some credential programs may give you a credential alongside another degree, such as a master's, but others will offer only the credential itself. This is something to think a lot about. Credentials are often necessary for certain career fields, but if you are unsure the field is right for you yet continue, you may find yourself with a credential that doesn't directly translate into other forms of employment. As with all degrees and all job fields, you'll need to match your experiences to the field you want to go into and learn how to make the case that the material you learned in a graduate program or in a job is a good fit for the new places you want to be. The upside to credential programs is that they are often shorter than master's programs, so you may be done in as little as one or two semesters.

WHAT YOU KNOW AND WHO YOU KNOW

I'm sure that at some point you've heard this saying: "It's not about what you know, it's about who you know." I've always hated that. For working-class people, this almost seems like an insult. To me it always seemed to imply, "No matter how smart you are, or how hard you work, you're never going to get into the club." I still feel that way to some extent, but like many things we encounter as first-gen students, if we can't change it, we must find ways to work around it or use the system to our advantage. It might sound strange, but as first-gen students, one advantage we have is that we often know that the system is set up against us from the beginning. As one of the first people in our social circles to go to college, we realized quickly that the systems around us were not built to make our lives easier, or to help us gain opportunities and resources. Instead, we often had to fight to search out whatever opportunities and advantages could be had.

Obviously this is a disadvantage, but if we go into this process *knowing* that we are at a disadvantage, we can be clear-eyed about what we need to do. We cannot count on our brilliance or our hard work alone. We have to plan, we have to strategize, and we have to make the most of every tool we have access to. By getting into college or graduate school, we have been given access to a powerful tool, and access to a lot of brilliant people who can give us insight and ideas about how the systems around us work and how we can use our education to our advantage. My instinct, when I was in grad school, was to focus hard on what was right in front of me: my schoolwork, my research, and my degree. That was fine, but it also meant that I was missing the access I had to a ton of resources around me that I could have used. I was lucky I found the job I did find, because I would have had a much harder time if I hadn't. Don't make the mistake I made. Take full advantage of what you have access to, while you have access to it—it will pay off.

SPECIAL NOTES ON THE PhD

I mentioned before that if you are at all interested in a PhD, you should be making it a part of your research project right now. Given that a master's degree isn't necessarily going to get you any closer to a PhD in the future, it makes sense to investigate a PhD now, not later. For many of us, a PhD can seem like an impossible dream, but the reality is that, more likely than not, you have all the skills you need to finish a PhD program now. Whether a PhD is the right choice for you is a different question. When you're making that decision, there are a few things about the job market for graduates with a PhD that you should know about.

Being a Professor

Before I came to college, my perspective on what it meant to be a professor was pretty much based exclusively on the movies and TV shows

I had watched and the books I had read that had professor characters in them. Those fictional professors worked in gorgeous old brick buildings and wore sport coats with patches on the elbows. They sometimes solved mysteries or hung out with high-ranking politicians. In those books and shows, professors were given a level of respect or even reverence by virtue of the position they held. It seemed special and almost magical, maybe like being a teacher at Hogwarts. I imagine that a lot of other first-gen students are like me, in that the only exposure we had to jobs like professor or doctor or lawyer growing up were in media we consumed. Where else would we get information on the larger world? Without people in our lives with those jobs, how would we know what it's like to be in such a position on a daily basis, let alone how they got their job or even how much they get paid? I said earlier that if you were able to get a bachelor's degree, you most likely have the skills you need to get a PhD. We must stop thinking about these higher degrees as unobtainable and instead think about them practically. In other words, you have to stop thinking, "There's no way I could ever be *X*," and start thinking, "I could definitely be *X*, but how can I find out about the reality of being *X* to see if that's what I actually want to do?"

I know this type of thinking will seem a little strange. If you're like me, you'll feel uncomfortable at the thought of sitting down with a professor and saying, "I don't know if I would want your job. Can you tell me how much you get paid?" I mean, you shouldn't say it exactly that way to anyone, but the mentality is the right one. We shouldn't put these positions on such a high pedestal that we can't look at them realistically. I know that when I was younger, the idea that I would even *think* I could be a professor seemed like a huge stretch, and talking about it as a plan made me feel like I was acting like a big shot, that I thought I was more important or special than I was. I know this is likely something that everyone experiences, no matter their position in life, but I do believe that those of us from working-class backgrounds are especially sensitive to the criticism that we are "forgetting where we came from" or "acting like something we're not." In other words, even thinking that we could achieve something like being a professor could get us accused of being pretentious or arrogant. But this attitude also means that we have extra barriers when it comes to trying to figure out if we even *want* to be a professor or lawyer or doctor. Who are we to ask someone in such a high position if they like their job, or how much time they get to spend with their family?

This attitude that gets ground into us can help keep us humble and grounded. It can also hinder us from making realistic plans about our futures or really considering what we can accomplish. I want to try and tackle this problem head-on and tell you some realities about being a professor. I'm not saying any of this to scare you away from a PhD, but I do want you to have some accurate information about what getting a job as a professor can look like.

Up front, let me say that being a professor is an awesome job, and I really love it. I get a lot of control over my own schedule; I have a good amount of freedom to teach the material I'm interested in and teach it in ways that I find the most useful. Being a professor gives me a lot of time to spend with my family, and while every job comes with stress, the stress of this job matches with my personality well. So, I love being a professor, but if I'm being completely honest, I need to let you know that I was extremely lucky to get the job I have now. A lot of graduate students coming out of their PhD programs don't get as lucky as I did in finding a job.

The reality on the ground is not encouraging. In recent years, the number of jobs for professors hasn't kept pace with the increasing number of newly minted PhDs, and public investment in higher education hasn't kept pace with the growing number of students going into the system. Meanwhile, university administrations have decided that one way to save money is to hire a lot more non-tenure-track professors on a part-time basis.

Basically, in U.S. universities today, you will be hired either as a tenure-track professor or as adjunct faculty. A tenure-track professorship is what most people imagine when they think of a typical professor's job: You're hired as a full-time employee by a university, placed on a type of extended probation period that can last up to five or six years. At the end of that period, if you've done everything the higher-ups asked, you apply to be promoted from an assistant professor to an associate professor. This promotion, if granted, is what we call tenure: It basically means that a person has passed the probationary period and been hired on a permanent basis by the university. Having tenure can be a great deal. You have a lot of job protections and, if you continue to do the things asked of you, will have a lifetime appointment at your college. How long that "lifetime" appointment is and how good the job protections are depend on your union (if you have one) and on who is in charge of the university and the government in your state. In many states in the South and the Midwest in recent years, governors and university presidents have decided to cut funding to higher education, and even tenured professors can be fired when an entire department is eliminated by budget cuts.

Despite these realities, a tenure-track job is still a good deal. Generally, the pay is good, though not amazing, and the benefits are usually good too, like being part of a state pension system and health care plans if you are at a state university. These details vary widely, though, depending on the university. Some universities, private or public, may pay less in salary and benefits than others, based on their location in the country and on union status.

The second type of professor job is the adjunct. This is just a fancy way of saying "part-time" or "contingent," which is a way for the university to pay someone less for what amounts to similar amounts of work. Contingent or adjunct faculty get paid a lot less, on average, than tenure-track faculty; they also have fewer benefits, and when budget cuts happen, contingent faculty jobs are the first to be cut. In other words, a contingent faculty member is typically in an unstable situation.

Adjunct faculty are paid a flat rate for each class they teach, not a salary. Often, contingent faculty are not given enough classes to amount to a full-time job, so many teach at a mix of university, colleges, and junior colleges to get enough work to support themselves. That can work out if you live in an area with multiple colleges or universities within commuting distance, but in a less populated area you'll have fewer options.

Being adjunct faculty is not all bad. As a graduate student, I taught a lot of classes at my local junior college and at the state college in my hometown. When I combined that with the income I was making from working as a teaching assistant or teaching a course on my PhD campus, it was enough money, when added to my wife's income, to help raise our small family. I really liked the people I met when teaching at the community colleges, and even though I was contingent faculty, I often found a lot of work and had other area colleges calling and asking if I was interested in teaching classes. It was great work for getting experience, but the lack of a consistent schedule from one semester to another was a source of stress. Also, in many departments, contingent faculty are not included in department decision making and can sometimes be treated as second-class citizens by other faculty or the larger university community. It's not that way everywhere—our department, for instance, includes all faculty, tenure-track or not, in our meetings and decision-making processes. But that is an exception to the rule, and in many cases, adjuncts are not a part of the department structure.

When applying for university jobs, many new PhDs find they can get a visiting assistant professor, or VAP, position. These jobs are a lot like being adjunct faculty, but instead of getting paid class by class, you are given a one- or two-year contract to teach a certain number of classes. Sometimes these contracts will be renewed at their end, but it's not guaranteed. I've known a few people who have shuffled from one VAP job to another, moving to a new university and sometimes a new state every few years. This is probably not a sustainable way to make a career or raise a family—well, for me at least. I'm a lot more comfortable with stability, but others may like the flexibility and variety that comes with this type of position. In many cases, people take VAP jobs hoping that it will put them in position on the front line for a tenure-track job when one opens. That can and does happen, but being a VAP in a department is not at all a guarantee that you will get the job. In some cases, being a VAP may work against you in applying for a job within the department. When a department hires new professors, they often want to see that they have a record of active scholarship they will carry with them into the position. Any department that wants to hire you will also want you to be successful in getting tenure, so if tenure requirements include research, the hiring committees will want to see that you will be able to meet that goal. The issue is that VAP jobs often come with high teaching requirements, sometimes asking a person to teach almost twice as many classes as tenure-track faculty. That doesn't leave a lot of time to get a research project off the ground. This can put you at a disadvantage compared to graduate students or new PhDs who have been spending their recent energy trying to get published and not worrying as much about teaching.

Working at Community Colleges

Many PhD grads go on to get tenure-track jobs at community colleges. But these jobs are not guaranteed any more than the ones at universities are, and there will be other PhDs competing for the jobs. Teaching at a community college as a tenured professor can be an amazing job, but you will be required to teach a significant number of courses. A normal teaching load for tenure-track faculty in a community college can be nine or ten classes a year. If you imagine twenty-five to thirty students per class, multiplied by five classes a semester, you're looking at grading 125–150 final exams and similar numbers of midterms, term papers, and class assignments over the course of a semester. It can be a daunting task, not to mention the organization it takes to keep all those courses and students straight.

I'm not saying all of this to discourage you. After a few years in graduate school, I started to see how the job market worked, and I made my peace with the fact that I may be an adjunct professor my entire life. I didn't necessarily want that to happen, but I had also decided that it was a risk I was willing to take to continue my education and have a job I really love in teaching sociology. I had worked a lot of different jobs in the past, and I knew that teaching sociology was about the only thing I liked to do. I also knew I was good at it. That was a good feeling, and if my family had my back, I was willing to live with costs that might come with not being in a tenure-track job.

What I want to get across here are the likely realities of being a professor and the job market you will be stepping into as a new PhD. For many first-generation college students, the idea of getting a PhD in the first place seems insane, so the reality is that we probably have no idea what the job looks like and what will happen after we get a PhD. As an undergrad, I saw my professors as almost godlike, in that they had done something amazing in earning a PhD—I assumed that such an attainment was rare and that they'd had multiple tenure-track offers to choose from. The part about doing something amazing in earning the PhD was true enough, but my ideas of their jobs and status were, again, based mostly on old movies and TV. I saw being a professor as an almost romantic profession: walking on tree-lined campuses past stately brick buildings, having an office with a fireplace and a beautiful leather reading chair. Those tree-lined campuses and old brick buildings exist in real life, but those few plum jobs at elite universities are extremely difficult to get, and grabbing one can be as much about how you play the game of academia as it is about how brilliant your work is.

PhDs AND NONACADEMIC JOBS

Now that we've talked about the realities of the job market with a PhD, we should talk about what you can do about it. If you are interested in going into a PhD program to be a professor, there is no reason to set that goal aside, but it would be a really good idea to also plan for a future in which you need to look for jobs outside of the academic world. People with PhDs go into jobs outside of the academic world all the time, but there can be some challenges to making a move like this, especially if it's not something you prepare for early in your PhD career.

In the private sphere, having a PhD can be seen as an awesome achievement that can help you get jobs in anything from data analysis to consulting to being the director of a nonprofit. But just as with a bachelor's degree, the degree itself will not go get you a job—it will be up to you to find ways to let people know what skills you bring to the table and to make a case for why you will be good in the positions they are hiring for.

Lost in Translation

In many ways, the process of going through a PhD program is an exercise in learning a whole new language. A PhD is a highly specialized academic degree, and to be successful you need to learn to speak the academic language of your discipline. This can be a huge challenge all on its own, but if trying to move into the *nonacademic* world after finishing the degree, many find that the language they spent so much time learning is one that people outside the university don't understand. Let me give you a slightly unrelated example. In my early twenties, I worked in the accounting department of a small tech company. It was small enough that there were only two of us in the department, so I reported directly to the CFO of the company, which sounds a lot fancier than saying I had a boss named Tammy who was the main accountant. Because we were a small company, Tammy and I pretty much did everything there was to do in accounting. I paid bills, sent invoices, put together reports, did a ton of filing and data entry—all the normal tasks you would expect for a business accountant. After two or three years at the company, the economy took a downturn and I was laid off. Afterward, I went to apply for a state job in an accounting department. I felt qualified—I had done the work for three years and I was decent at it. But when I went in for the interview, the person across the desk asked me if I had ever done "reconciliation." I was kind of stumped. I wasn't sure if I had ever done reconciliation. I was pretty sure I had, but I was just guessing at what the term meant. I had to ask them to explain and they seemed surprised. I realized that this was probably a fairly common term that larger accounting departments used, and they were kind of shocked that I had no idea. I didn't get the job. Later I looked up what reconciliation was and realized that I had done a ton of it, we just never called it reconciliation—we called it "double checking the books." That difference in language cost me an opportunity.

As you make your way through to a PhD, you will learn all kinds of specialist language that other academics in your field use constantly. Consider how you would translate that language for a friend or a family member. That friend would not know most of the jargon you use in your program, but if you were to put it into common terms, they would probably have a sense of what you were talking about. The same applies to job opportunities outside the academic world. You are going to have to work to translate your skills and experience for other people who don't speak your professional language.

To make things even more complicated, many professions you may be trying to go into have their own types of professional language that you may not have learned in school. If I had known what *reconciliation* meant in accounting, I might have had a better shot at that job. If you go in knowing some of the terms that are common in the field you are applying to join, you will have a better shot too. So where can you learn the language? The only way is to research, study, and talk to people.

I know that this sounds like a lot of additional work, on top of what you will already be doing to earn a PhD, but like other degree programs, your PhD program is just training for a career—it will end eventually, and you will have to go out and find a job. The more you incorporate that idea into how you spend your time in your PhD program, the better your results will be.

Fortunately, most PhD-granting universities have a lot of resources that you can take advantage of when working on translating your skills for people outside your academic world, and for gaining access to people you can talk to about the job market. These universities have connections to the job markets through career centers, research centers, alumni centers, and more. In many cases, you may never need to interact with these resource centers during the normal course of earning your degree, but it will be worth your time to get familiar with them, talk to the people who work there, and use them to start making a plan for what you will do with your degree after you graduate, whether you plan on pursuing an academic job or not.

When I was working my way through the PhD program, I was all-in on becoming a professor or instructor at a university. I spent my time almost exclusively on my program and on teaching and didn't spend a ton of time making connections outside that world. Again, I was extremely lucky that this worked out for me; for a lot of people who were in my program, it didn't work out like that at all. One of my friends in the program, once she finished, decided that the academic world was not for her and quickly realized that she was going to have to find a job outside academia. It took her a lot of time and energy, after receiving her degree, to find out how to speak the right language and to translate her skills in a way that employers would understand. In addition, she had to learn to navigate the system for applying to state and other jobs in California. All of this meant time, energy, and stress well after her PhD was in hand, not to mention a period when she was bringing in little income while searching for a position. Luckily, it worked out for her: She found a really good job in a state department that valued her skills, gave her an opportunity to do meaningful work, and respected what she brought to the table. But the process of getting there was rough.

Compare her experience to that of another friend who was also in our program but who always had an "open to anything" attitude about where she might end up working. Because of that attitude, she was constantly exploring opportunities outside our department for work and other connections, including with people at our university who had worked with the federal government, which led her to more opportunities for grants, travel, and employment. As she worked on her PhD, she was also learning how to translate that work and the skills she was gaining to a wider audience. When she finished the program, she had several connections she could rely on in pursuing job opportunities. She ended up working for a department in the federal government, doing amazing health-related work. Both of my friends found interesting and important jobs in the end, but the first had to endure a lot more stress along the way.

WHAT'S NEXT?

Now that we've had time to think about different career paths, different degrees, and hopefully a little bit about ourselves, we can move on to researching which schools and which programs will be the best fit for our goals. Next, we will go over how to research different universities and different programs, what to look for, and where to get the most reliable information.

6

RESEARCHING SCHOOLS

WHAT IS YOUR RADIUS?

A mistake that students make every year is to consider only grad programs at the institution where they are already enrolled. I get it. If you're a first-generation college student, you've most likely put a lot of time and energy into understanding the written and unwritten rules of the institution you are a part of. It makes sense: You wouldn't want to do all that work over again, so staying at the university where you've already learned the ropes sounds better than starting from scratch in a different institution. That's not wrong, but it's not the best way to think about the possibilities ahead of you. If you pick a university first, instead of an area of study, you are limiting your possibilities and constraining your imagination to the programs that university happens to offer.

Another issue is that grad school applications are a numbers game, and there are often more applicants than open seats for a given program. This means that the raw odds are not necessarily in your favor. We go through a lot of things in this book that can help you tilt those odds, but most programs are not going to accept everyone who applies, so there is always a chance you won't get in. If you apply to only one program, you limit your chances of acceptance enormously. It's like playing darts with the goal of hitting a bull's-eye and allowing yourself to throw only one dart. You might make it, but the odds of hitting a bull's-eye go up the more darts you throw. From this perspective, the best strategy would be to throw as many darts as it takes until you hit the target.

Practically speaking, we are limited by time, money, and energy in how many schools we can apply to. None of us can apply to every school that offers the degree we are looking for, but we should start with the goal of locating every possible program that we could attend within reason if we were accepted. A good way to think about this is to find your "radius"—basically, the farthest distance you could practically commute to or move to if you were accepted to a program. For some of us the radius will be wider than for others. I had a student once who didn't have many limitations in terms of personal commitments. When she thought about her radius, it was basically only limited by her travel budget and her ability to support herself wherever she ended up, so she applied to a PhD program in Edinburgh, Scotland, and was accepted. That was an extreme case, but the logic is the same for everyone. If you don't have many personal commitments that are keeping you in the place you are in, your radius could be three hundred miles or three thousand.

For most of us, though, family, work, and life commitments mean that we are limited in our ability to just pick up and move to another city, another state, or another country. If that's the case for you, then you need to think about the practical distance you *can* travel. If moving to another state won't work, what about another city? If that would be too much, then how far can you commute in a day if you need to attend classes two or three days a week? The distance you arrive at with this calculation is your radius. You can use that measure to draw a circle around where you live, stretching out the distance you calculated in all directions. Once you draw that circle, look at what neighborhoods, cities, counties, or states are in that circle. Our goal is to locate any university in that circle that offers the program you are interested in and add them to the list of possible applications. Once a school is on that list, our job will be to go through the list and make a spreadsheet of each program that answers the questions laid out in the next section.

The size of your radius will depend on a lot of personal things in your life. For instance, right now I am limited by the need to drop off and pick up my kids from school. My travel in a day is limited to the places I can reach between those two hard deadlines. What your radius is will come down to your own personal circumstances and the time and movement constraints those commitments place on you. No matter what those circumstances are, our goal is to get as many programs as possible on the research list. The more schools we can include on the list, the more chances we are giving ourselves to hit the bull's-eye. Even if you aren't quite sure how you would make a particular commute work right now, you should still include that program on the list of possibilities. We can always take it off later, or even turn down an acceptance, if we decide that we can't make it work. For now, even remote possibilities should stay on the list. Trust me when I say that even schools you aren't really excited about now will become a lot more interesting if you get an acceptance letter. Suddenly, the place you never wanted to live in, or even visit, starts to sound like an interesting possibility when the reality of being accepted hits, especially if other options haven't worked out.

For some of us, the radius will include only one school. Family or work responsibilities will sometimes mean that even a shorter commute just isn't feasible. If that's the case, don't worry, there are a lot of people in the same circumstance. And there are options. First, consider closely whether the university you are applying to offers more than one program that may open the doors to your career goals. If you are interested in being a social worker, for instance, it may be smart to consider applying to a counseling program at the same time. Applying to multiple programs at the same school is a great way to give yourself multiple chances. However, if there is only one university and one program that fits your goal, you need to be prepared to apply more than once. This is true for everyone—we all need to make plans for what happens if we don't get in—and we'll discuss this more in chapter 12. But having just one shot means preparing to repeat the same application process as many times as necessary.

No matter what your radius is, don't forget that grad school is not a destination; it's a small part of the journey toward your larger goal. Even though getting into a graduate program seems like an enormous task right now, you are attempting this whole process only to achieve something more. Commuting to a school or moving to a new city will be inconvenient, for sure, but the two years you spend getting the master's degree, or even the six you spend getting a PhD, will ultimately be a short amount of time, compared to how long you will work in your career. Even if this means you need to apply two years or more in a row, once you are in the program and on your way to the career you want, you'll realize that all the time you spent getting there was well worth it.

WHAT TO FIND OUT ABOUT EACH PROGRAM

After you've determined your radius, your task is to locate every university within that radius and start researching the schools and programs they offer. At a minimum, your goal is to make a spreadsheet that covers the basics about applying to each program you might be interested in. Remember that your goal right now is to include as many possibilities as you can, not to write off programs for one reason or another.

For each program you've identified, research the following at a minimum:

- Application due date
- Tuition cost per semester or per year
- Fee waiver
- Application cost
- GRE required?
- Prerequisites?
- How many letters of recommendation?
- Transcripts: official or copy?
- Minimum GPA and GRE (if applicable)
- Offers online classes (all/some/none)?
- Course schedules (day/night/mix)
- Statement of purpose, letter of intent, or CV?
- Out-of-state tuition?
- Other programs that may be of interest?

WHERE TO GET INFO

The checklist information is the minimum you want to know about each program, but there are many other things you will want to know before you apply to a program, and especially before you commit to attending a particular university. In this section, we'll cover sources of information that you can use to help you find out more than just the basics about the programs offered at each university. I won't waste your time telling you to research the programs online. Most of us have become internet experts by virtue of being alive. My eight-year-old knows more about tech than I did by twenty, so I'm sure I don't need to tell you anything. I will give you some tips, though, on places to look that you might not know about and ideas about who to talk to.

Office of Graduate Studies

Every university that has graduate programs should have a page on its website for its office of graduate studies. Basically, this office is the administrative headquarters for all the grad programs on a given campus. You can use the website, and visit or contact the office, to get general information about graduate programs on the campus, other insights about being a student there, and a list of all the graduate programs the university offers. The website likely has links to every graduate program, from certificates to PhDs, on the campus. This can be especially useful if you are trying to think about what degrees you may be interested in, or alternate degrees that can potentially put you in the same career field. You may already have a particular degree in mind, but using this list can introduce you to programs or degrees you never knew existed or give you new areas of study to investigate. At the very least, I recommend browsing through the grad studies web page of every university within your radius and looking through the programs they offer. The office of graduate studies is also a useful source of contact information for each of the programs on campus. Remember: *When in doubt, talk to a real person.*

Department Web Pages and Grad Coordinators

The department web page can be a great place to get basic information about a program and how to apply to it. I will caution you, though, that department web pages can often be confusing, and sometimes they are out-of-date. Remember that you are dealing with academics, not web programmers. We often decide to change something, and it may take weeks, months, or even years before the department web page is updated. We generally don't have an IT person who works directly in our department and instead rely, in many cases, on student interns (who we think know more about computers) to update our pages or make important changes. I'm not saying don't trust what's on a department web page, but if you ever get conflicting information from one page to another or in different documents, you need to talk to a real person. Don't try to figure out which deadline is the real one on your own—*ask someone*. I am emphasizing this because I have enough experience as an introvert to know that a lot of us would rather do almost anything than talk to a stranger on the phone or email someone for help. This can be a big mistake that can cost you. If it's important, don't rely on a website. Talking to someone in person is the way to get the most reliable and timely information.

Departments often offer information sessions, in person and online, about their programs. These can be extremely valuable to attend. The people presenting are often professors in the program itself and can give up-to-date information that you may not find on the website. One word of caution, though: I have met with a lot of students who have come away from information sessions intimidated and discouraged about their chances of getting into a program. While info sessions can be great, there is also some incentive for professors at the sessions to emphasize how exclusive their program is, how many people apply each year, how few spaces they have available, and other things that may make you feel like your chances are low. Professors in these situations can't give personalized assessments of your individual chances of getting into a program, so they give a general sense of who gets in. Often, when we hear that description, our attention is immediately drawn to areas where we believe we don't measure up, and then we attach higher significance to those areas than to others. Don't use general, broad statements about who is accepted to judge your chances. Instead, talk to your mentorship team, who are in a much better position to give you an honest assessment. Also, don't forget that no matter how many people apply each year, a good percentage of them will be last-minute applicants, who may not have had the kind of time or energy that you had, to put in the effort and care that will show in your application. If you can set aside the time, energy, and overall attention to your application over the course of a semester, your package will automatically stand out from a big chunk of the others.

Grad Handbooks

One resource to look out for when researching graduate programs is a document called a graduate handbook. As an undergraduate, your college has a catalog that lays out exactly what you need to do in order to graduate with a degree in your major. The equivalent for that at the graduate level is the grad handbook. It tells you exactly what the department requires of you for graduation, including the courses you'll be expected to take from one semester to the next, the tests you'll need to pass, and the major research papers or other projects you'll need to produce. In many cases, it will give you a timeline of "normal" progress through the program and what students are expected to accomplish each semester.

The grad handbook can be a great resource for thinking about whether a particular program is a good fit, both for you as a person and for your lifestyle. Many first-generation college students enter their grad program with a job, a family, or other nonacademic responsibilities. It can be crucial to think through how the expectations of the program can match (or not) with the responsibilities of your life outside grad school.

First, list the classes that all students need to take in their first year in the program. You should be able to look up the class schedules from the previous semester to see what days and times they were offered. It's not guaranteed that they'll be offered at the same time in the semester that you start, but most likely they will be offered in a similar time slot. If you check through the schedule in multiple semesters, it will give you a good idea of when the class is most often offered, and you can get a pretty good idea of what your first- and second-semester schedules will look like in terms of days, times, and total hours. This can be important if you will need to coordinate work or child care with your class schedules. If you are still deciding what schools to apply to, you can use this information to find out if a program offers courses only during normal school hours or if they have night or weekend classes, or even online versions of required classes.

When you know what courses you will need to take, you can also ask the program administrator for a syllabus from each. Collecting a syllabus from a professor for a course they teach is a pretty common practice, so no one should look at you funny for requesting one. The syllabus can reveal useful information about the level of work and, just as importantly, the *type* of work you'll be expected to do, and whether a particular set of classes is going to be a big challenge. Looking at a syllabus beforehand can give you other clues as well—if you are someone who really doesn't do well on multiple-choice tests, for example, you may learn what professor *not* to take a class with.

Another thing to look for in the grad handbook is major milestones in the program and timelines for hitting them. This can be a big deal, so don't overlook it. Planning out the stress of a big undertaking like this is one way to help you get through it. Many programs will require a research paper or an extended internship. If you know the timing in advance, you can plan the rest of your life around these milestones. Giving your employer a heads up, planning a vacation that coincides with a big test, or arranging with family to have child care coverage a few months ahead of the paper you need to write can help you manage the stress you'll be taking on. Remember that grad school is as much about long-term planning and project management as it is about being the smartest person in the room. People who are prepared and who can build support systems will succeed at a higher rate than people who have only their own brilliance going for them.

Lastly, the handbook should give you a sense of what to do when things are going wrong. Many programs include leave-of-absence policies, grade change or grade appeal procedures, and even instructions on how to change advisors in the grad handbook. If a program has taken the time to set up policies and procedures to help students when something goes wrong, it's a good sign they're prepared to help you through tough circumstances. If it seems, instead, as if they haven't even considered that life may at times interfere with a student's ability to perform well, that may be a sign to reconsider whether this is the program for you.

Just as in all your other research, make sure to really take your time reading through the handbook of any program you want to apply to. I know that taking this much time to consider a program when you aren't even sure you'll get in may seem a little presumptuous, but your mindset going into this entire project should be that you are planning for what happens *when* you get in, not *if*. With that in mind, remember: This process is about you picking a program that is right for you, just as much as it is about a program picking your application and letting you in.

A Note About Sources of Information

You're about to be a college graduate, so I know that the following has been covered in classes you've taken. However, I've talked to enough of you over the years to know that this is something that needs to be repeated and put in all caps: NOT ALL INFORMATION IS GOOD INFORMATION! Not all sources of information are created equal, and you can't believe everything you read. I know I sound like I'm giving a talk to my son about how he can't trust everything he sees on YouTube. You already know this. But every year, I see people stumble because they get information from a source and then forget to check it against other sources. I see this the most frequently when students find information on a website or hear it secondhand through a friend. This can result in missed deadlines, using bad information to decide, or just flat-out missing opportunities.

So where do you go if you need good information about a program, about a career, or about choices you are considering making about your future? Let's go through a hierarchy of information that will clarify where you can get it and when you can trust it.

THE INFORMATION HIERARCHY

1. Person who works in the field or program

FACE TO FACE The absolute gold standard for information is talking in person to someone who works in the field or directly in the department you need information about. If you want information about what types of degrees are needed to get a certain type of job, talk to a person who has that type of job. If you are confused about an application procedure or requirement, go talk to the person in the department who oversees handling that aspect of the application (often the graduate coordinator). Notice that I said to talk to these folks "in person." The best source of information is a face-to-face conversation. A lot of information is conveyed when you talk to a person face to face that can be confused or misinterpreted when you communicate by phone, text, or email. Take it from someone who has been married for twenty years—a lot can go wrong in an email, where intentions and meanings can be easily misunderstood. Talking to someone in person is the highest level of information gathering, and it is also the highest level of priority. If you need information *now* and you're on a deadline, showing up in person will give you the best chance of getting that info. Phone calls can go to voice mail, emails can get lost, sent to spam, or just outright ignored, but showing up in person will mean that someone is going to have to deal with your issue. I'm not saying to be weird or pushy or a stalker. What I'm saying is that students often use email because it feels safer—showing up in person can make you feel uncomfortable and exposed—but know that when you need important info on a timeline, showing up in person makes you much harder to ignore and greatly increases the chances you will get the answer you need.

PHONE CALL OR EMAIL Most of what I wrote above applies here. Talking to a person who works in the field by email or phone is the next best thing to being with them in person. The source is the same, though you may be slightly easier to ignore if you are emailing or calling. This may be the only option if you are geographically distant from the person you need to talk to. Information received directly from a person who works in the area you need info about will almost always be better and more relevant than info from a website.

2. The internet

WEBSITE OR WEB PAGE OF THE DEPARTMENT OR UNIVERSITY YOU ARE INTERESTED IN I know that this will be the go-to for most of you, so if you are getting most of your information through internet research already, go to those places first. When we research grad school, there are a lot of sites that have general information about grad schools generally or about the field we are interested in, but that info will always be less accurate than info from the department itself, or at least from the university. If you can't find the answer on the department web page, call them—or better yet, show up in person.

Let me give you a quick example. A regional state school near me has a master of social work program. On the website, they list a prerequisite requirement for all students who are applying to have taken a class in child development. Many students I have worked with have written off this entire school from their research list because they had not taken a class called "child development" during their time as an undergraduate. However, when we contacted the department, it turned out that a variety of classes could fulfill this requirement, even if the words *child development* weren't in the course title. The online information was correct, but there was nuance that wasn't conveyed on the website. When in doubt, call someone.

GENERAL INTERNET SOURCES I'm not one of those professors who say to never use Wikipedia. It can be a great jumping-off point to get you started on a research project or to point you in a good direction for sources, but don't trust information from Wikipedia or from any other web source that isn't directly connected to the career, the job site, the university, or the department that you are interested in. If anything, use Wikipedia or other general web sources to point you in the direction of people you can contact directly, and get info from them.

3. Friends and other relations

This is the lowest tier in terms of reliable information. Sometimes, your friends or other people you talk to may have good information about a program, about a career, or about a decision that you are considering. However, if they aren't directly connected to the career or the program you are interested in, then you need to double check everything they tell you. I can't tell you the number of times that students have given me wrong information, with complete confidence, that they got from a friend or another student. It's not that these sources are malicious, it's just that they often don't have the whole story or are missing key pieces of information. The students I talked to were sure that the information they had received was correct, so they didn't bother to follow it up or check in with a higher tier of information.

OTHER THINGS TO CONSIDER

One question that comes up continually in my graduate seminars is whether it is worthwhile to apply to online programs or to private colleges. There can be a lot of things to watch out for when you are considering each of these options, and we are going to go through some of them here.

Public Versus Private

Colleges and universities typically come in two varieties: public institutions, funded and run by the state they are in; and private institutions, not directly connected to the state government. There are many excellent state universities and many excellent private universities. The most famous universities that most of us have heard of through TV shows and movies are typically private, like Stanford, Harvard, or Yale. However, for every private institution you've heard of, there are a hundred more you haven't heard of. For instance, when I was attending San Diego State University, not too far away was the University of California, San Diego (UCSD), which was also public, and the University of San Diego, a private Catholic university. It can be confusing, trying to tell them apart and figure out which type of institution is your best bet.

One major difference between private and public institutions is cost. States set the tuition and fees of public institutions, which were often founded in part to educate people who didn't have the money to attend private schools. Private colleges, on the other hand, can charge whatever they want in fees and tuition. In my state, the University of Southern California (USC), one of the premier private colleges, charges close to $70,000 a year in tuition, while the public university where I work charges closer to $8,000. That's close to a tenfold difference, but it's an extreme example—not every private school is as expensive as USC. Financial aid is available to students in both public and private schools.

The real question is whether the difference in cost is going to be worth it—that is, returned in the value of the degree you will earn.

Aside from the cost difference, there are other potential issues you should be aware of when considering a private university. While many private universities, including USC, have excellent reputations and provide an amazing education, there are other sorts of private institutions that are more interested in collecting your tuition dollars than in providing you with the skills you need. I'm sure you've heard of predatory colleges. These are institutions whose goal is to get you in the door, get you registered for classes, and collect money either from you or from financial aid. Once they've managed that, you may find you're on your own.

Colleges in this category can seem like a godsend in many circumstances. They often accept students more readily than other institutions—for example, by admitting students for the spring semester rather than requiring them to wait until the fall. They may also offer an easier path to a degree that is impacted (see the glossary) in public institutions, promising that you'll be able to start your career sooner and not have to cross your fingers for admission into a state program. In California, many of the nursing programs in our public colleges are impacted and it can be difficult to get in. However, if you are willing to pay three times the price of a state program, there are almost always seats available at a for-profit college somewhere not far from you. This is a big problem. It's possible that it's worth the increased cost if it means starting right away and being able to get into your career field sooner. But how do you know that the institution is going to provide a good product for your money, provide support, and help get you across the finish line?

In this situation, with chronic high prices and the rise of predatory schools, we need to be extremely cautious and do a lot of research. Online can be a great place to start, but your research can't end there. Talk to as many people as you can about the schools that you're considering. Talk to the professors in your current institution and see if they have had any experiences with those schools. Try to talk to current students in the programs you're researching and see how they feel about the institution. They can give you really valuable inside information about the program, how it supports students, which professors to work with and which to avoid, and a general feel for how students view the institution. I've heard stories of programs where current grad students would warn potential students to stay away because of how poorly they were being treated. You may have to do some extra work to find current students to talk to, but that effort can really pay off.

Another *big* one, as always, is talking to people who currently work in the field you are interested in going into. Have they heard of the program you are considering? Is a degree from that institution respected and accepted widely in the field? These would all be great things to know about before you decide.

I don't mean for the caveats about private schools to make them sound scary. There are some great private schools that I would completely recommend, and I know several students who had good experiences at schools I had never heard of. Those students did their research, talked to a lot of people, and made a decision that worked out for them in the end. I just want to make sure that you have all the information you need before you jump into a program that could end up being enormously expensive.

After all that concern about private schools, how about state schools? Aren't there predatory or unsupportive state schools out there? Couldn't they be just as bad as the exploitative private schools mentioned above? To quote *The Simpsons*, "Short answer yes with an *if*, long answer no with a *but*." Some state schools may be unsupportive and generally to be avoided. However, because state schools are not run for profit, their tuition and fees will usually be nowhere near as high as those of private institutions, and they are generally not looking just to get you through the door and paying. If you are considering a state school, you should do the same types of research suggested for private schools. Talk to people, get a feel for the level of support, but overall, your level of caution can be slightly lower, knowing that the programs don't exist solely for the purpose of turning a profit.

Online Programs

Online programs can seem like a godsend. For those of us who have needed to work our entire college careers, or who have family or other responsibilities, the allure of being able to mold our school schedules around our existing time constraints is very tempting. I'm not here to tell you to avoid online programs altogether, but I will say that there are some things that you need to consider before you enroll.

KNOWING YOURSELF

This one is big enough that I have a whole section on it later in the book. Knowing yourself, your work style, and how well an online program fits is enormously important. Often, online classes will move at your pace, meaning that many of the courses will not have a set time where you will need to log in and be present. For some people that will be amazing—they will be able to listen to a lecture after the kids go to bed or on the weekend when they have a break from work. But I have taught enough classes to know that when work can be put off until later, it will be put off until later.

For many students, having flexibility will mean repeatedly pushing assignments back just a little longer, because something more urgent has come up. The issue is that when the deadline isn't a deadline, anything else becomes more urgent. In a way, deadlines can be useful because they help us organize our time and our priorities. No one likes the pressure of having a due date creeping up on them and causing anxiety, but when the due date is "by the end of the semester," other tasks take precedence from day to day. The work we need to do is continually pushed away, into "next weekend," and then "next week," until suddenly the big deadline of the semester's end is staring us in the face and we have multiple papers, quizzes, and other assignments all due at once.

If this sounds as familiar to you as it sounds to me, you should think long and hard about whether you will have the ability to quickly unlearn all the study and time habits you've built up until this point and become someone who can diligently stick to a schedule without the pressure of a ticking clock.

Another thing to think about is the difference between face-to-face interactions and the disconnected nature of courses online. Learning is a tricky thing and is different for everyone. I learn best in circumstances where I can ask questions, talk through examples, and raise issues when there is something I need clarified. The physical gap between you and instructors can make this more difficult. Think about the best classes you've had so far as an undergrad. What are some of the things they have had in common? If your answer includes class discussion, group projects, talking with the professor, or other aspects of in-person learning, just be aware that many of those elements will be very different in an online setting. For me, online courses—both when I'm teaching and when I'm a student—can feel alienating. I don't feel as connected to the material or to class. Feeling this way makes it tough for me to be passionate about the work I'm doing or stay motivated. If this sounds like you, you should probably earn your graduate degree through an in-person program.

Online programs *can* be an excellent fit for some people. I've known quite a few students who are great at setting a schedule, keeping up with their work, and staying motivated to engage with the class, even though they never see the instructor or other students in person. For some, these things are the reasons they love online courses. If this sounds like you, number one, tell me your secrets to being an organized and competent human being, and number two, you'll most likely do well with internet-based classes.

CONNECTIONS

One of the biggest parts of a graduate education is making connections with other people, both professionally and personally. Connecting with professors can be enormously beneficial when you are attempting to learn difficult material, but it can also be a huge help in building the networks you will need to rely on when you go out looking for a job. Just as you will need letters of recommendation for your grad school applications, you will need professional letters of recommendation when seeking jobs in your new field. Professors are a great place to start for all of this. In chapter 4, we discussed building a mentor team as you start the process of your applications, but that project starts all over when you get into a program and begin your PhD education.

Peer networks are another huge resource, but one we often take for granted. Every year, I teach an internship course at my university, and every semester, people find interesting places to intern because another student in the class made an announcement, or a friend who had taken the class previously recommended an organization. These peer networks also exist in graduate school, and may be even more valuable there in terms of helping people find job or internship opportunities, or even just talking about which professor is a good mentor or should be avoided.

It's not that these exchanges can't happen in an online program, but in my experience, it's harder to build both mentor and peer relationships over the internet than in person. An online program will most likely offer you ways to connect with other students, but if those students are in other cities or states, sharing information about the job market becomes tougher. It makes building relationships with professors a little harder too. Don't get me wrong, people can build meaningful connections over the internet and through Zoom calls or FaceTime. I talk to a therapist every few weeks whom I've met in person just once, and it's worked out great. But speaking as a professor, communicating *only* through the computer greatly narrows the range of our experience of each other as people and limits some aspects of our ability to communicate. It's harder to build trust through a computer screen, and harder to build empathy, both of which are critical to a good mentorship relationship.

LOCAL OPPORTUNITIES

This may matter less if the job market you are applying to is national or international—for instance, if you are in a PhD program and you could be applying to jobs all over the country or even overseas. However, if you are going into a field in which local connections are important, an online program will mean that you will have a lot more responsibility to build those networks. If your professors are in Arizona and you are in Georgia, it will be tough for them to tell you what your local school districts are looking for in educators, or point to a good internship site in your town.

It's not impossible for an online program to make good inroads with local institutions. I've worked with students who had success doing online social work programs that helped them connect with internships in their own city. If your program involves being connected to local community resources, it is important to find out how well the program does in placing students at sites that are far from the university itself.

PREDATORS

Unfortunately, for-profit universities know that students may be more likely to sign up for classes if they feel that they can work those classes around their schedule. Since this is the case, many of the predatory colleges may offer more online programs than other universities—and, given that for-profit colleges often have entire departments devoted to recruiting students, the "salespeople" for the university can do an excellent job convincing you that their program will be the easiest fit for your schedule. And as when considering private colleges in general, you will need to raise your level of scrutiny when looking at online programs. That said, an online program offered through a state school is probably a safe bet, though you should still do your homework. But a private online program calls for the same level of research I recommended for private schools, plus some added attention to things like retention rates, job placement, and student support.

In the bigger picture, doing an online program can be a really rewarding experience, and for some people it may be the only way that a graduate education is possible. If this is you, don't let the things I said in the last few pages deter you, but instead just go into the research and application process with your eyes open, knowing that being disconnected would mean extra work for you over the course of your graduate education. If you plan, you can anticipate and deal with many of the disadvantages of an online program and not miss a beat after you graduate. Just remember, the key to doing well in an online program is time management and communication. You need to be in constant contact with your professors and the program administrators. So much information can be lost when communication isn't happening face to face, so be sure to check in frequently and always ask questions.

SUPPORT SYSTEMS

Something I've noticed over my years of being a first-generation college student and teaching other first-gen students is that there is usually a pattern in how many of us approach new and intimidating situations. Starting college with no real previous experience of what that means or what will happen when you're there is an overwhelming experience. I've come to see that many students take the same approach to these situations: We keep our heads down, we try not to stand out or draw attention to ourselves, and we try to do as much as we can to understand the situations we are in and the institutions we are a part of. Asking questions draws attention to us, and it's a natural response to not want others to see you as having less information or as incompetent. In many instances, we assume that other people all understand what's happening, so if we ask questions, we'll be singled out as the person in the group who is slow or behind the rest.

There is good reason to want to avoid those circumstances. A lot of sociological research has shown that being labeled as a slow learner or a troublemaker has an impact on student outcomes, and often this label can carry over from one teacher to another. Any of us would have good reason to want to avoid that reputation. The result is that we often try to blend into the background as much as possible, to avoid revealing that we don't know much about what's going on and what to expect.

There are some other positives to this reaction. It can lead us to do extensive research on our own, trying to decipher the systems that we are going to be a part of before we encounter them. This is a great habit, and if you are planning for graduate school, then chances are that these habits have gotten you this far and have worked well up to this point. However, I'm here to tell you that those same habits of keeping your head down, not asking questions, and avoiding standing out can just as easily work against you as you move forward. In fact, those same habits can lead to a lot of problems when we expect that our research has told us everything we need to know about an institution and all the steps we need to take to get to the next level or to graduate. I can't tell you the number of times I've sat down with students who have skipped advising meetings because they were intimidated but thought that by doing all their research online, they could map out their graduation plans, only to let them know that they were missing a critical piece of information that threatened to extend their time.

When I was an undergraduate and about to finish my senior year, I realized there might be things I needed to do in order to graduate, other than take classes. I was assuming there would be a form to fill out and that would be it, but what I hadn't counted on was that the university took up to a semester or more at that time to process a graduation request. When I found that out, I panicked. I was applying to graduate programs that were going to want to see that I had graduated with a bachelor's degree, and if my application was still being processed, it might mean they wouldn't accept me. I went to the chair of my department for the first time in my three years at CSU Sacramento. He took pity on me and made a phone call to the administrative building, where someone put a rush on my application as a favor to him. By thinking that I had all the information I needed and trying to avoid the pain and exposure of an advising visit to a person I had never met, I had almost shot myself in the foot and screwed up my graduation.

Hopefully, I'm doing a good job convincing you throughout this book that even though reaching out to people in your university, in your community, and in your peer group may be painful and trigger that fear of exposure that so many of us feel, it is also an *essential* part of being a successful graduate student. You need help! And more than that, you *deserve* to be helped in your journey. Most of those you reach out to will be kind, empathetic people who will do their best to help you get where you need to go, but the one thing they can't do is know you need help before you ask.

What does that mean in terms of the types of support systems you are going to need when you go on to graduate school? From my experience, there are a few different levels of support that you need, and finding allies at each level is extremely important.

Academic Level

This one is straightforward: You need allies at the teaching level of your university. Find professors who are willing to talk with you, give you a heads up about policy changes, help you improve your writing and research, and help guide you through the steps of the program you are in. Professors will be the first people who will be able to write you letters of recommendation, give you ideas and insights into career fields, and hopefully offer encouragement along the way. These relationships are a little easier to build than some of the others because professors have office hours during which you can visit them, they teach classes you may be taking, and generally they are accessible to most any student.

Administrative Level

This one is a little tougher, because people who work in admin don't typically meet regularly with students, aside from occasionally providing some information, paperwork, or assignment. But being on good terms with key administration people will make your life *way* easier in your grad program. Most programs have a person called "graduate coordinator" or a similar title that indicates they handle all the administrative issues for the program. This person probably knows more about how the program works at a nuts-and-bolts level than anyone else besides the department chair—and a graduate coordinator who has been there long enough probably know more about the inner workings of the administrative side of the university than the chair does.

The work you put into getting to know this person, or at the very least being friendly, will absolutely pay off in the long run. You don't need to be weird about it, just be sure to be friendly, remember administrative professionals' day if you can, with a card or a coffee, and generally do your best to be kind. Admins can make your life in a program so much easier or, on the flip side, a nightmare. Being on familiar terms with the people who will be handling the day-to-day aspects of your education, including your paperwork, records, financial aid forms, and so on, is always a good idea.

Additional Support

This is another crucial aspect of your time in graduate school. Hopefully, your university will offer several extracurricular support programs that can help make your time in there easier, and your transition into your field much smoother. Examples are places like the career center, academic advising, the multicultural center, the women's center, health centers, and more. These places exist on campus to help you through the process of earning a degree and moving on to a career—but you need to *reach out* to them to take advantage of what they have to offer. Many of these centers offer tours, information days, or open houses. Do your best to plan these into your schedule and go to them. These centers typically have only the resources they need to run their programs—advertising their existence to students or actively seeking out students who may need their help is not something they have the time or money for. This means that the onus is on you to go find the services that will help you the most and to take advantage of them.

Let me give you an example. During one of my later years in grad school, I found out about a new grant that was going to be given to one grad student in each program on campus. It would fund the recipients for an entire year, without requiring them to teach a class or be a teaching assistant. This would be a gold mine, allowing the student so much more time to write and prepare than if they had to teach a class. I heard about the grant through my peer groups on campus, and even though I was sure I wasn't going to get it, I applied. Well, I did get it, but not because I was such a genius or so amazing that they absolutely had to give me the grant. No, it was because only two people applied for the grant in my department and I was the closest to finishing my dissertation, so they reasoned I would be able to make the best use of the extra time. Either no one else had heard about the grant, or others had been intimidated just as I had been and had counted themselves out of the running before they even applied. Looking back, I can tell you that there were probably a lot of opportunities that I missed out on because I had convinced myself that I wasn't qualified, I wasn't competitive, or I wouldn't measure up for some other reason.

Another quick example. In my second year of being a professor, I was asked to help judge an undergraduate student research competition the university was hosting. When I showed up to judge the contest, it turned out that only three people had submitted proposals in the social science category that I was judging. Since we had four cash prizes to give away, every person who was brave enough to apply got at least $250. If one more person had given themselves enough credit to even try, they would have gotten the same amount by default.

Finding these opportunities is on you, and it's also on you to take the step of applying for them—and believing in yourself enough to put yourself in the vulnerable position of asking for help or taking the risk of being judged. If my experiences have taught me anything, it's that we should never disqualify ourselves from opportunities that might benefit us. We must not let our assumptions about ourselves keep us from trying for opportunities that we are completely qualified for, which would only take us out of the running before anyone has had the chance to see our work.

FINANCIAL AID

Funding graduate school is a huge deal, and you should do a lot of research about the school you are going to and the associated costs. There are also some misconceptions that many students, first-generation especially, have about the costs of graduate school that I want to cover here, and information on what financial aid might look like.

First, you need to know that you are not necessarily on your own in paying for graduate school. Many people believe that financial aid ends with their undergraduate education, but that is not the case. What is true is that the *type* of financial aid available often changes. The major program that students take advantage of during their undergrad years is the Pell Grant, and some states offer supplementary grants for undergraduates. In California, it's called a Cal Grant. Those programs are only for undergraduate students and won't follow you into graduate school. However, there are other grant programs that do apply to graduate school and that you may be eligible for. Unfortunately, it is also true that grant programs for graduate school can often be less than the amount of support you received during your undergraduate program, but there are a few factors that may help to offset this. The first is that when you were an undergraduate, if you were under twenty-four, you were required to list your parents' income on your FAFSA application. When you apply for graduate school, you are automatically considered financially independent, so you won't have to list that income anymore. For many of us, that's good news. The income limits for programs like the Pell Grant often mean that they expect parents to shoulder a large part of the cost of college, but just because the federal government does a quick calculation about your parents' finances and finds them to be substantial, that doesn't necessarily mean that your parents can afford to pay thousands of dollars in tuition for you each year. Now that you are applying to graduate school, their income won't be considered, and if you are like most undergraduates, you make considerably less than your parents, so this change may increase the amount of grant money you are eligible for.

Second, many schools offer grants for their graduate students that are in addition to any grant money you may get from the federal government. This can be an important thing to find out about when you are applying, so be sure to talk to someone about programs that are available. Also, if you are applying to a PhD program and are accepted, most schools will offer you what they call a "financial package," which is basically a job. For most PhD students, the job is a teaching assistantship or a research assistantship that requires about twenty hours a week. The job will pay you money each month, but it will also waive your tuition, meaning that essentially you will be paid to go to school. I had no idea this was the case when I was applying to graduate school—I just imagined that I was going to have to fund the whole thing through loans. When I found out that I was going to be paid, I was in shock. Why had no one ever told me this? Why was there so much about the process that I was finding out only *after* getting accepted? It was a nice surprise, but it also highlighted how much I didn't know.

Third, schools will have scholarship programs you can apply for. I know that a lot of you don't want to hear about scholarship programs. Whenever I heard that I might be able to fund some of my education through scholarships, I always thought, "Sure, I can also buy lottery tickets and maybe I'll win enough to pay for tuition. That seems about as likely as getting a scholarship." I won't tell you that this attitude is wrong per se. It's true that scholarships are a type of a gamble—they are often competitive, and it's always a guessing game as to what scholarship programs want to hear from candidates.

All these factors lead students to see scholarships as an unlikely means of support, and they're not wrong—but they're also not right. No matter what you think you know about the likelihood of getting scholarships, there are important things you don't know. For one, you don't know who is going to get them. You have no idea. You also have no idea how many other people felt discouraged in the same way you do and never applied. In reality, although scholarships are not a reliable basis for long-term plans about your college financial goals, they can be totally worth the effort it takes to apply. And after all, you are already doing a huge amount of the work that it takes to apply for a scholarship just by applying for graduate school in the first place. You are already writing essays, and you are already prepping your other materials, such as your CV. The additional work of a scholarship application may be as little as a few edits to your personal statement and the time it takes to fill out your name and address in the online application portal. Our pessimistic views about our chances for scholarships may not be misplaced, but they can lead us to not take chances on things that have a possibility of paying off. Yes, applying for a scholarship is a type of gamble with no guarantee. However, it's also a gamble in which the cost is relatively low and the potential reward is high.

The odds against us may not be so great anyway—we don't have a solid way of assessing the real odds of winning a scholarship because we have no idea how many other people are applying. It's true that for many scholarships, there will be a lot of other applicants and many of them will be extremely overqualified people with awesome GPAs. However, we have no real way of knowing beforehand which scholarships are going to get a ton of applications and which aren't. We also don't know the criteria that each scholarship program will use from year to year to choose their recipients. Yes, it's probably true that a person with an amazing GPA will have a better chance of getting most scholarships, but you also have no idea if a particular program in a particular year is looking for some qualification that you happen to have. It's pretty much impossible to tell. So, in a situation where the potential benefits are high and the costs to apply are relatively low, it can make a lot of sense to apply to any and every scholarship you think you might have a shot at, and even some you are convinced you have no hope of getting. They may all turn out to be rejections, but it's 100 percent certain that if you don't apply, you won't be getting a scholarship. So just apply!

Student Loans

In my conversations with first-generation students, I've noticed that most are very cautious when it comes to student loans. Given that the past few decades have been filled with horror stories about predatory schools and insane debt burdens that people sometimes never find their way out from under, it's completely understandable. The best outcome for anyone is to get out of their education owing nothing, but for many of us that is not realistic.

There are some basic things you should know about student loans going in, including the different types available and how to strategize about possibly using them to fund graduate school. One major issue that often scares students is the potential cost of grad school. As mentioned earlier, for most programs, especially in state schools, the price of graduate tuition should be similar to the undergraduate tuition. That means that for most state programs, you are likely not looking at owing the price of a small house when you get out of your program, but even if you financed every dollar you needed in graduate school, it would be more like the cost of a used Toyota. That's not nothing, and no matter what the cost, all students should take the prospect of debt very seriously. However, the scare stories we've all heard about students owing enormous amounts of money are usually in the context of private universities where tuition can run between $50,000 and $60,000 or more a year. With that price tag, it would be easy to get very deep in debt very quickly. With state school tuition averaging around $8,000 to $10,000 a year, a two-year master's program may not be quite as financially scary as a four-year degree from Harvard.

Generally, there are three types of loans that you might have access to as a graduate student. The first two are administered through the financial aid office, as an option in the FAFSA process: federal subsidized loans and federal unsubsidized loans. The difference between the two is basically how much you will have to pay back in the long run. In both cases, the loans give you the money up front to pay for tuition and possibly for living costs and other expenses. Typically, you are not expected to start repaying these loans until roughly six months after you graduate. Let's look more closely at the differences between the two. With a subsidized loan, the money you borrow will not start accruing interest until you begin the repayment period. That's different from something like a credit card, where you will be charged interest pretty much immediately, which increases the amount you will need to pay back over time. You won't be charged any interest on a subsidized loan until after you graduate, which could save you thousands of dollars in the long run. With an unsubsidized loan, interest starts once you receive the money. Even though you don't need to start repayment until you graduate, the amount of money you owe will be slowly increasing while you are in school. Obviously, subsidized loans are the way to go if you have a choice. Having the interest not start until repayment may end up saving you a lot of money, so if you need loans, these are the best ones to get.

How much you qualify for in subsidized or unsubsidized loans will depend on some secret formula that the financial aid system uses, and your best bet, if you want to plan in that direction, is to make an appointment to talk to someone in the financial aid office. They won't be able to tell you specifically how much you might qualify for, but they should be able to give you ballpark figures that you can use in your planning.

Repayment

Repayment of federal loans comes with a lot of options that most people don't know about. Most federal student loans offer various repayment plans, including plans that are based on the income you are making. If you aren't making a ton of money after graduation, your monthly repayment amount should be low. If you make more later, it will be higher. Repayment terms are often spaced over a pretty long period, sometimes as much as ten or twenty years depending on the plan, so even if you do owe a full used Toyota's worth, the amount you will need to repay each month won't necessarily be comparable to a car loan that is repaid over four or five years. The interest rates charged on federal loans are often relatively low, and way lower than on something like a credit card.

There are other advantages to having a loan through the federal government. There are several ways these programs will work with you if your circumstances change, if you lose a job, or if the repayment amount is becoming a problem. During the COVID-19 pandemic, my wife lost a job. Since our loan repayment amount was based on our two incomes, I called the repayment office and told them what was going on. They sent me the forms right away to report new income so that we could get the amount adjusted. The service rep also paused my repayment for three months so that the adjustment could go through and I wouldn't have to pay a higher amount in the meantime. No credit card company has ever offered to do anything close to that for me.

I do have to add one caveat, though. I originally wrote this section in the fall of 2024. Since then, there has been some degree of change in the financial aid situation. Like any government program, financial aid can and will get caught up in battles between politicians and political parties. Unfortunately, one party has lately been using financial aid to try and stir up a backlash against some of the forms of student debt relief that were offered in the COVID period and its immediate aftermath. You, I, and many others will potentially pay the price of this political wrangling, if and when major changes to the financial aid programs are made. The best way to get a good idea of where you stand is to talk to someone in your financial aid office directly—at your home campus, and potentially at any university that you are interested in attending. Even in political turmoil, your best weapon is information. The more information you have, the better your choices will be.

Debt and Trouble

None of the previous information implies that loans are free money or that you won't have to pay it back. You will, and you can get yourself into an excessive amount of debt if you aren't careful. Often, you will be offered money in student loans that can be extremely tempting to take, if only because it will make life easier in the short term. When I was young, I had no real clue about finances. I knew I needed to go to college, but I also knew I was broke. It all added up to a bad circumstance in which I took out more in loans than I needed to pay for tuition and books each year, and I got myself into quite a bit of debt. Because my grades were not great, I didn't qualify for the Pell Grant, so loans were my only option. The extra money helped me cover gaps that my job couldn't cover, but taking on so much debt was not a good idea. Student loans are easy to get into but difficult to get out of. Thanks to our wonderful politicians in Washington, D.C., student loan debt can't be discharged in bankruptcy, so if you take the money now, you will have to pay it back later.

I don't want to scare you, but just let you know what can happen and that you need to be prepared and careful. Research is the best way to avoid a costly mistake. Research the average pay in your state for jobs you are interested in. Talk to people who have the kind of job you want and ask them how much they make. I know that asking about money is considered rude or distasteful in American culture, but this is information you need. When determining how much debt you may need to take on to get a particular degree, you should factor in how much money you stand to make, or not make, once you get into the career field you are aiming for.

Private Schools and Private Loans

A third type of loan is available to students: the private loan. I've already talked about private schools and the new twists they add to our calculations about graduate school. That applies to financial aid as well. If you get into Stanford, that is a major accomplishment, but when you see how much you will need to pay to attend, your excitement will be dampened a little. Financial aid can absolutely help cover the cost of a private school, but usually financial aid has set limits for how much it will pay per student, either through grants or loans, and if that amount isn't enough to cover the tuition of the school you were accepted to, you will be asked to cover the rest out of your own pocket.

These circumstances can often make private education loans tempting. Banks will advertise these loans to you constantly while you are in college, and if you search Google for financial aid, be prepared to be bombarded with ads for loans wherever you go online. Private loans often come with some terms that are similar to those of federal student loans, but they also come with some really important differences that can cost you a lot of money. First of all, private loans will most likely not be subsidized. Just as with federal loans, they will not ask you to begin paying the money back while you are in school. But unlike federal subsidized loans, most private loans will be charging you interest on that money the entire time you are in school and not paying back the loan. That means that once you graduate, you have been accumulating several years' worth of interest and the balance on your loans will be significantly higher than the amount you borrowed. Additionally, since private banks are in the business of making money, they are also likely to charge higher interest rates than loans through financial aid. All of this means that the dollar amounts can grow pretty quickly.

The other major difference with private loans makes them much more like credit card loans than financial aid loans: The terms of repayment are typically set in stone, you will be held to making regular payments of a certain amount whether you can afford it or not, and the bank you borrowed the loan from will be very unlikely to pause your repayments if you lose a job or experience some other major life change.

At the very least, you should be extremely careful when considering private student loans. For some people who can't cover the gap between the price of tuition and what financial aid is offering, private loans may be the only option. If that is the case, you should take a very serious look at exactly how much you will need to borrow, what your likely payments will be when you finish school, and how much you are likely to make from the job you are potentially going to have. You need to be extremely practical about this before getting a private student loan. I strongly advocate to my students that having a job they love will often make up for not making as much money as they otherwise might, and it may also justify big loan payments. However, if you end up owing so much money that you have a hard time making ends meet, or so much that it seriously compromises your ability to have a sustainable life outside of work, that will put a big strain on your ability to love the job you are in. Stress is stress, whether it comes from work, from finances, or from family life. Our goal is to put you in a situation where your stress from work is offset by the fact that you enjoy what you do and feel fulfilled by it. If we add a significant amount of financial stress on top of that situation, it may change the equation in a big way.

Funding a PhD

When I first decided that I was going to pursue a PhD, I resigned myself to the idea that I was going to need to go into a lot of debt to do it. I had found my experiences working in normal office environments so horrifying that I was willing to take on any cost in order to join the academic world. I had no idea that most PhD programs come with their own funding sources that are separate from financial aid, and when I was actually accepted into a program and they sent me a letter that contained a "financial package," I just about fainted.

In fact, most PhD programs at major universities offer funding to their incoming students, often guaranteeing them funding for multiple years. This will usually be in the form of grants that cover tuition and fees and some kind of job or scholarship that covers a stipend paid to you for living expenses. To me, the idea that someone would *pay* me to go to school was about the best thing I had ever heard, and even in hindsight I think it was a really good deal, but there are some details you should know about the financial package that many PhD programs offer.

How Long Is Guaranteed?

One big consideration is that PhD programs can often last multiple years—sometimes as few as three, but often six, seven, or more. Universities will often guarantee funding for several years, but the number of years offered may not cover the average time to graduation. What then? Usually, there will be opportunities to find additional sources of funding once you run out of guaranteed years. In many programs, TA (teaching assistant) positions, RA (research assistant) positions, and even teaching jobs will still be available to students who are out of guaranteed funding, and these will cover your fees and tuition and provide a stipend. It's a good idea to talk to any prospective university about how much funding they will be offering you and how long it takes their average student to graduate. If the time to graduation is significantly longer than the guaranteed funding, you'll want to ask them how current students cover the gap, and then talk to some current students to find out how that's working for them.

How Much Will You Be Paid?

The answer to this question can vary pretty significantly from one university system to another. In some systems, like the University of California, the TAs and RAs are unionized, so the pay and benefits are collectively negotiated and standardized. When I was a grad student, this meant roughly $2,000 of funding a month and health care that covered me but not my family. That was in 2014, though, and things have probably changed since then in terms of pay and other details. Other universities may not be unionized, so your stipend, your benefits, and other details may vary from department to department or may even be up for negotiation. This can sound great, but in reality, as a student you are not in a great position to negotiate, so talk to other students to find out where you can push for more and where you can't. A sympathetic faculty member you can trust as a source of insider information could also be a huge help.

More to Consider

There are a couple other things to consider when you think about PhD funding. The first is that the funding that gives you a stipend is usually in place only while you are actively a TA or RA, which means that you may not be getting paid during the summer. There may be summer jobs available at the university, but those are usually not a part of your guaranteed funding. When I was a student, the summer positions were somewhat seniority based and students who had been there longer were more likely to receive them.

Another thing to consider is that as a freshly graduating college senior, the amount of money being offered through the stipend may be more than you were earning at the job you had been working up until that point. This can be really exciting, but consider that you will likely be making this amount of money over the course of your time as a PhD student and that the amount may not significantly change from when you start to when you finish. The amount of money being offered can be great when you are younger, but as you get older, take on more obligations, start a family, or see your friends who have full-time positions earn more each year, the money will start to seem a bit tighter. How much tighter will vary with each person's circumstances, but likely your level of enthusiasm for the amount of money being offered up front may be somewhat lower by the time you finish.

None of this information is meant to be discouraging. You just need as much information as you can get if you are going to make a good decision. The more you can talk to current students, financial aid staff, and faculty, the more clear-eyed you can be in planning for your future.

Some Good News for All Students

Now that I've given you some of the more sobering news about student loans, let me give you some news that may offer a bit of relief. There are several programs that may help you deal with the burden of student loans, depending on the field you are going into. The federal government has a program that will allow you to write off student debt after ten years if you work for a nonprofit. Since many first-generation students will be going into fields that involve nonprofit organizations, this may mean that even a larger student loan burden won't last forever. The main program is called Public Service Loan Forgiveness; it has terms and conditions, so look carefully and see if you qualify. Many states operate their own programs that offer similar loan forgiveness or grant programs. California offers some incentives for people going into teaching, and other states may offer programs that you qualify for.

Talk to Someone ASAP

The best source of information on financial aid is the financial aid office itself. Even if you plan on attending a different college than the one you are at now, you can make an appointment with the financial aid office at your current institution and talk with them about your plans. They should be able to give you general ideas about what you may qualify for, whether there are grant programs or scholarships you may want to pursue, and whom you can talk to for more information. I will note that occasionally, you'll run into someone who is less than interested in helping you. That may be anyone from a professor to a financial aid officer. The important thing is to not let this slow you down. You must continue to push through, even after a discouraging meeting or encounter. If one financial aid staff member is less than kind or generous to you, try again with another person. If you can't find a helpful person at your school, try a local community college or call financial aid customer service directly. What you cannot do is allow the bad luck of running into someone who's having a bad day, or is just not in the mood to be helpful, redirect your actions going forward. One person being a jerk is not necessarily an indication of how someone else is going to treat you or of how that entire office or department receives requests. I've worked with many students who have let a bad encounter with one person derail them from getting the information they needed. Remember, persistence is the key: You have to keep knocking on those doors until you get someone to respond.

ON TO YOUR APPLICATION!

The research step can be a lot of work, but the more thought you put into the programs you apply to and the universities you want to attend, the more prepared you'll be, and that will show in your application. If you spend the time to find out exactly *why* you want to apply to a program, your materials will have an edge over those from people who are just applying to *any* program. It makes a difference. Now that you've done that part, we can start getting into the mechanics of the application itself: how it works and how to be sure you submit something that paints you in the best possible light.

PART THREE

THE APPLICATION

7

STARTING YOUR APPLICATION

THE APPLICATION ITSELF

Many students assume that applying to graduate programs will be pretty much their undergraduate application process all over again but with a few changes. This isn't the case. You need to be aware that there are some big differences in terms of how you apply to a graduate program versus how you probably applied to your undergraduate institution. When you applied to the latter, you were applying to the university as a whole and either selected a major or left it undecided. Your application most likely went to the admissions office, where the same group of people processed your application alongside everyone else's, no matter what majors they were interested in. This is not the process when you apply to be a graduate student.

Instead of applying to the university as a whole, you are essentially applying directly to the department you want to be a part of. (This can be more complicated for PhD students, who often are applying not only to the department, but also to work with specific professors who will be their mentors, lab heads, dissertation chairs, and so on. We will talk more about this in chapter 11, on letters of recommendation.) Instead of your application going to the university admissions office, it goes directly to the department of physics or psychology or whatever, where a committee made up of professors and sometimes of grad students in the department evaluates applications. This is important for a few reasons. The first is that if you meet the minimum requirements, a person with a direct connection to the department you want to study in will be reading your application. This is good news for most of us, because it gives us a chance to showcase exactly why we would be a good fit for the program we are applying to. Unlike a university-wide admissions department, the department admission committee will be reading far fewer applications (though still a lot), and that means more of a chance that someone will read your essay as if you are a real human being and not just a collection of scores and grades and numbers on the other end of a computer screen.

We'll talk about how to take advantage of this in chapter 8, but for now what you really need to know is that each department gets to set many of the rules and requirements for admission into their graduate program. These can include things like due date, GPA requirements, types of materials they want, and more. This means that what materials you need to submit and when they're due can vary not only from one school to another, but even from one department to another in the same university. So, really be on your toes in terms of your research into each program. I mentioned earlier that we gain an advantage for each additional university and program we can apply to, but this also means that we need to research each department we apply to as its own separate entity. You can't assume that if you apply to two departments in the same university, they will require similar materials or even have the same due date.

Chapter 6 includes a list of things you should research about every program you are interested in. Basically, if it's in your radius, you should do this minimum level of research as a first step. We can always cross programs off the list later, but if we don't do the research now, there is always a possibility that we miss a program due date down the road that we didn't know about.

WHEN TO APPLY

The question of when to apply is a little trickier than it first appears, but most programs will list a deadline, and you should do everything in your power to make sure that your application is submitted on or before it. Also, there are some situations that come up from time to time that you need to consider.

Deadlines

Most programs have a due date by which all your materials need to be in. The deadline is pretty much the drop-dead date, and you absolutely need to have everything in by the deadline . . . well, kind of. Often, programs have some leeway to allow for delays in receiving items like transcripts or letters of recommendation. In many cases, they will not throw your application in the trash if a transcript takes a few days longer than expected to arrive or a letter of recommendation from a professor hasn't been uploaded before midnight on the due date. However, these same programs may be less forgiving when it comes to the parts of the application that are strictly up to you to submit. When you are planning your timeline, you should give yourself two weeks of lead time, which means planning for a deadline that is two weeks earlier than the deadline posted on the website. Set everything up so that you are ready and in the process of submitting your application on that two-week-early deadline. There are so many technical issues, small snags, and last-minute questions that can come up that you are really pushing your luck if you wait until the due date to upload all your materials while crossing your fingers that nothing goes wrong.

This is also a good deadline to give to your letter writers. In most cases, your letter writers will be given a log-in to a letter portal that will list a submission deadline, but it doesn't hurt for you to give them a deadline that is a little earlier just to help move things along.

Early Applications

Students always want to know if applying early is a good idea. In most cases, there really isn't a big advantage, outside of a few exceptions. The department will typically wait for the deadline to pass, then start the process of reviewing all the applications that came in. Some people might start reading some of the applications early, but for the most part the actual discussions of the candidates and a full review of the materials won't happen until after the deadline. The people reviewing the material are professors, who are likely more concerned with end-of-semester grading and their upcoming winter break than with getting an early start on your application.

As I mentioned, there can be exceptions. If a program states that they will review applications "as they are received" or that they have a "rolling admissions" process, there is a real possibility that they review each application upon arrival. If so, submitting early may offer an advantage. If the department is doing that, there are more spots open earlier in the process, and thus you could potentially be competing against fewer applicants. As the open admission period rolls on, the number of spots starts to decrease and the number of applications gets larger—so there is a distinct advantage to submitting as soon as possible. However, a *good* application is better than a *fast* application. If submitting early means that you are going to be submitting first- or second-draft work, really think about whether it makes sense to submit early.

Another instance in which it may make sense to submit early is for scholarships or grants where a limited pot of money is handed out as applications come in—getting in later may mean that the money allocated to that scholarship or grant will already be gone. I've found this to be true for fee waivers, but I've also seen it happen with other grant programs. The key in both instances is getting information as early as you can. If you can do the research early in the process—the summer before or even earlier—you will have an idea about which programs and which grants you need to apply to first to be as competitive as possible. Remember, not all the programs or grants will be specific about which of these methods they are using to review applications, so when in doubt, *ask*. Refer to the information hierarchy and *talk to someone.*

Rolling Admissions

I wanted to give this its own section because I've noticed that there is a higher instance of "rolling admissions" in predatory programs. Rolling admissions basically mean that there is no set due date and that a program will consider an application when it arrives and make individual decisions that are not based on a deadline. That may also mean that students can be admitted in the fall or spring semester, depending on when they submit their application.

Predatory programs have an incentive to make the application process as easy as possible. When people are considering going back to school to earn an advanced degree, the process is daunting and often the application deadline is a long way off. If they find a school online that promises them that they can start courses right away and that they won't have to wait until December or January to apply, the prospect becomes more tangible and applying seems a lot easier.

These types of schools often have recruitment offices that will contact anyone who submits information through the school's website, and they are trained to tell you exactly what you want to hear. They will tell you that you will be accepted easily, will get financial aid, and can start ASAP. That can sound amazing to people who are dealing with the uncertainty and self-doubt that this process can bring up. These schools need recruiters for a reason—they are for-profit institutions, and they need bodies in seats to make profits. Be careful with these types of programs and do your homework!

This is not to say that *any* program that offers rolling admissions is predatory, but predatory programs often advertise this method. There are some legitimate schools that offer rolling admissions, but the key, again and as always, is doing your homework. If a program is easy to get into but the price is significantly higher than that of similar programs, this should send up a red flag that you need to do a lot more research to make sure this program is legit.

WHAT ABOUT GPA?

First things first: Everyone thinks that their GPA needs work. Often the students who are the most worried about it have a GPA I would have killed for as an undergraduate. So, no matter what your GPA is, chances are that you think it's too low and that this is an obvious reason why no school will ever want you in their program. It feels this way, but it's not true. I'm saying all this because year after year, I find that students are the most worried about their GPA, but often it is not the thing they should be focused on.

A better way to think about it is this: If your GPA meets the minimum requirement for the programs you want to apply to, there are diminishing returns to focusing on getting it higher. If you have above a 3.0, most programs will consider your application. If this applies to you and you are already in your final year, I highly recommend using most of your time on other aspects of your application, like your statement of purpose. The higher above a 3.0 you are, the less of a return you'll likely see in relation to the amount of work you will be putting in to get your GPA higher. What I mean by this is that at 3.0 or above, your chances of getting in will most likely depend less strictly on your GPA and more on your other materials.

If you meet the minimum requirement, someone is going to read your application, and that is where you will have the chance to shine. A GPA is just a number, and after reading ten or fifteen applications those numbers start to blend together. A 3.25 is not going to stand out in a major way from a 3.45, but a good essay will stick in a reader's mind where a number will not.

Some Notes If Your GPA Needs Work

There are several strategies you can think about using if you decide that raising your GPA will help your application. I'll go through some of them below, but first consider this: The more credit hours you have, meaning the more classes you've taken, the less your GPA is going to move with each additional grade. If you have over a hundred units already, each A is going to move you up only about 0.03–0.05 grade points. From this perspective, changing F's or D's to A's or B's by retaking a class or even changing a failing grade to NC (No Credit) can provide a much bigger boost than adding an A from a new class. For instance, if you have close to 120 units, changing an F to NC can boost you by close to 0.1 grade points. Going from a D to an A can get you nearly the same boost. If you have below a 3.0, targeting F's and D's may make the most sense for raising your GPA. What I'm trying to say here is that when considering ways to raise your GPA, the idea is to work smarter and not harder, targeting the easiest and quickest methods first and then deciding if it is worth it to pursue some of the more time- and effort-intensive methods last.

Another thing to consider is that your overall cumulative GPA is not your only GPA. Almost all programs will ask you to list your cumulative GPA, and some may also ask for the GPA for your most recent sixty units, or your major GPA. For most students, the GPA they earned over their last four semesters of college is a lot higher than the GPA they earned in the first few years while they were figuring things out. Make sure to find out exactly what GPA the programs you are applying to are going to consider with the most weight. If your overall GPA is 2.7, but the program you are applying to is most interested in your GPA over your last sixty units, and that is 3.4, you may not have as much work to do as you think. Additionally, we will talk in other chapters (on the CV and the personal statement) about ways to let your readers know that your overall GPA is not the only way to judge your academic performance.

The following are some things to work with in raising your GPA, including strategies for those with particular GPAs and ways to think about what your GPA means.

F Grades

As crazy as it seems, F's can be the easiest place to target for a GPA boost. I'll talk about F strategies in order of lowest effort to most effort.

ACADEMIC RENEWAL Many schools, especially community colleges, have a program whereby you can apply to have F grades removed from your record if enough time has passed. How much time needs to have passed will vary from institution to institution, so it can be worth the effort to check with a college you have an F from and see if they offer a way to have the grade removed from your transcript. If they do, great! Once it's been removed, resubmit your new transcripts back to your current institution (if they are different colleges) and you should see a good GPA bump once the F is gone.

CHANGE AN F TO NO CREDIT This one relies somewhat on the good will of departments or larger institutions, but if you received an F for a class, you can ask the instructor if they are willing to change the grade to NC. No Credit grades are awesome because they don't count against your GPA. This effectively erases the F from your transcript. In the Cal State system during COVID, we started loosening the restrictions on when students could change their grade to NC. The problem was that not all students heard about the policy and many took an F when they could have easily received a No Credit if they had known. In these instances, you have a case to make to the instructor or the department that you should be allowed to retroactively change the grade because of COVID or other extenuating circumstances. If you message the instructor of the course and you don't hear back within a few weeks, reach out to the chair of the department and see if they may be able to help you. The worst they can say is no, but in my experience, they are often willing to help.

RETAKE A CLASS If your schedule allows for it, retaking a class for which you received an F may be a great way to help undo the damage. You do need to retake the same course, but you don't need to take it from the same instructor. You can always do some research to see if another professor fits your learning style better and if you can take the course from them instead. This option often scares students because it puts them back in the headspace of the student they were when they failed the class. What you need to remember is that you are not the same student who did poorly in the class the first time around. For many students, it has been a while since they took the class, maybe even years. By now, they have a lot more experience under their belt and a lot of tools to use that they may not have had before. For other students, there were other extenuating circumstances that led to their failing the class. What happened one semester doesn't necessarily have a bearing on what will happen in the next. You are coming into the class fresh, and if life cooperates you will be able to pass the class.

High-Effort Strategies

Taking additional classes at a community college can be a great option if you have some time, but taking classes at your current institution is going to be too expensive. Any class that you take for units can transfer to your current institution and will impact your GPA. If you're close to graduation, you probably have well over a hundred units, so your GPA won't shift much. But if you're right on the line between 2.9 and 3.0, a couple of tennis classes over the summer might be just what you need to push you over the line.

Strategies by GPA

3.5+ Number one, I hate you. You have an amazing GPA, and you definitely do not need to stress about getting it higher. Your biggest goal is to stop worrying about your GPA and focus on other aspects of your application. Putting more time and energy into your GPA is probably not going to net a big return. If there are low-effort things to handle like getting rid of an F, go ahead and do it. But some of the higher-effort strategies are probably not a good use of your time.

3.0–3.4 Congratulations, you meet the GPA requirements of most graduate programs. That means that if you submit your application, they will read it, and that's where your hard work, planning, and preparation will pay off. There may be some benefit to doing some GPA work if it is low-effort. What I mean by that is to aim for the lowest-effort strategies that are listed. Changing F's to NC's or removing them is your best bet. If that isn't a possibility, then unless you have multiple semesters to work with to retake a class or two, your best bet is to concentrate on the classes that you have left, do the best you can, and put your time into your application materials.

2.5–2.9 This is the area where I would start to consider some of the higher-effort strategies. You need to pay extra attention in your research to the GPA requirements of the schools you are applying to. Do they require you to have a particular overall GPA, or are they more interested in your GPA over your last sixty units? What is the minimum, and can you find out the average GPA of the students they accept? All this information can help you weigh the time and effort you put into changing your GPA. If getting it above 3.0 is feasible before you apply, then that would be a good place to put your energy. If not, then focus on the schools where you meet the minimum requirements and plan on revisiting your GPA if you need to reapply the following year.

BELOW 2.5 This is the range where you should make the GPA your major focus. Don't stress out. At one point, my GPA was below 2.0 and I was asked to leave San Diego State (joke's on them, I'm smart now). In this range, we need to think practically about a mix of all the available strategies and focus on getting you into the 2.5+ range before we start focusing on graduate school. If this is your GPA range, then hopefully you'll be able to identify the classes where your attention will pay off the most.

None of this is to say that GPA doesn't matter. It absolutely does. However, the question is *how much* it matters and *how much* effort we should be putting into trying to "fix" your GPA. If you are in your final year, there's not a lot we can do *right now* to change your GPA, and if your GPA already meets the minimum requirements for a program in your radius, that program should be on your list for consideration. If you've not yet reached your final year, focus on doing as well as you can in your classes, and hopefully that will be reflected in your grades. It's true that some graduate programs weigh GPA more heavily than others, but how that calculation works, what weight is given, and how the individual people who are reading your application will interpret your GPA is out of your control. Your goal is to control the things you can control, and do your best not to worry about the things you can't control.

GPA Shame

One last thing. I've worked with so many students who feel embarrassed or ashamed about their GPA. When doing advising sessions, I've even had students who apologized for their GPA or, even worse, avoided talking to me altogether because they feared being judged. That's a natural reaction. If we feel that we are going to be judged for something, we are less likely to seek help or want to talk about it to others. Often, part of being a first-generation student is hiding that we don't always know what's going on, and feeling anxiety that we don't measure up to other students. You have to push back against this instinct. GPA is not a judgment of your worth or your potential. It's only a number, and like all numbers it can be manipulated, changed, nudged in one direction or another. Your professors and other advisors can often help you find ways to work your GPA into shape, but not if you don't talk to them about it first. As with so many things, there is help for you, no matter the circumstances, but you'll need to take the first step.

BUDGETING: IT'S A MARATHON, NOT A SPRINT

In fact, the entire process of applying to programs and getting ready to start graduate school is a marathon. Sprinting will never cut it here. I saw the difference recently when my son's elementary school had a "jog-a-thon." The school raises money by having the kids use their cuteness to get friends and family to donate money to "sponsor" them as they run laps around the school. The whole thing seems like a scam to guilt families into giving money to the PTA, but maybe that's just me being cynical. Anyway, the kids were over-the-moon excited, and when the teachers blew the whistles to start the twenty-minute run, some of those third-graders started sprinting like a monster was chasing them. I'd love to be eight again for a couple days. Those kids were flying around the field at a drop-dead run and looked happy to do it, showing off for the parents whenever they passed the cheering section on the far end of the field. For most of the kids, though, that enthusiasm lasted for about one lap. Then it suddenly dawned on a lot of them that they were supposed to *keep* running, even though they had just gone all-out for sixty seconds.

You could really see the distinction when the kids passed us on lap two. Some of the more athletic ones were still running like Usain Bolt, but the mere mortals started to get red faces, sweaty foreheads, and a little look of panic as they started to realize how long twenty minutes actually is. By lap three, the heroic speed bursts had all but stopped, and even though many of them still tried to sprint bravely past the parents' cheering section, they dropped into a heaving, shambling jog as soon as they turned the corner. One kid, though, was different. He started out running but not sprinting. He basically ran the same pace the entire twenty minutes. When other kids were burning out and bending over, hands on knees, after the first few laps, he just kept moving on down the track, not super-fast, but super-steady. By the time the race was over, he had lapped most of the other kids at least once, and it seemed like he could have run all day if he needed to.

In our quest to go to graduate school, we really need to learn a lesson from that kid. I've worked with a lot of people whose instincts are to pour themselves into the process all at once, taking all their excitement and energy and letting it propel them through as much of the process as they can get through all at once. If you are one of those people who seem to have an endless amount of energy, maybe this is a good strategy for you. But for the rest of us, what ends up happening is that we burn through that nervous, excited energy pretty quickly, and when we hit a roadblock, we lose a ton of our momentum because we're tired and we haven't conserved enough energy to get past it.

Budgeting Your Energy

Many of us got a burst of energy when we first really decided that grad school was what we were going to do and committed ourselves to the application process. There were a lot of things to do, but it all seemed fresh, exciting, a new challenge to be taken on. The biggest issue came when we got through all the easiest stuff—initial research, conversations with professors, uncomplicated preparations. But when we hit a piece of the project that felt more challenging, like the personal statement, confusion and uncertainty started to slow our momentum. Running into a speed bump like this can be devastating if you've been sprinting through the entire process so far. A sprint requires a burst of sustained energy, momentum, and fluid, fast movement. But it's over pretty quickly. Much more like a marathon or cross-country running, the application process demands a longer, carefully paced, more creative feat of endurance and tenacity. Sprints take place on flat ground or a simple slope, but a marathon may take you through hills and valleys, on roads but also on tougher terrain. If you spend your energy going all-out on the easier flat stretch, you won't have much left when you encounter the first hill.

Practically speaking, you are going to need to pace yourself and plan your time and energy wisely. We are used to finding ways to budget our money and our time, but budgeting our energy is a skill that not many of us have. Looking at my kids, I realize how much of their day, especially in their early years, is spent being high-energy and happy or tired and angry. I've been yelled at by enough preteens to know when someone needs a nap and a snack—and once I've had both, the kids have usually run out of energy to scream at me. I'm kidding, but the reality is that this feast-or-famine attitude toward your energy use leads to burnout. That's a problem when many of you are going to be facing the end of the fall semester, finals and term papers, and now you're adding applications to the mix. You don't have time to spend a week recovering from pushing yourself past your own limits time after time.

Now is a great time to start to think about your own energy cycles. How have you handled periods of high workloads and high stress in the past? Do you wait until the last minute and use the panic as a motivator to get through the work that you must do? Have you had any luck splitting up work over a longer period and doing things one piece at a time? Does having a big project to do seem unmanageable or are you able to split it into smaller tasks? All these are skills that don't just come naturally to a person—they need to be developed and practiced. The nice thing is that these are also skills that you are going to need both in a graduate program and in a future career. The more you move on in your education and in your career, the bigger and more complex the projects become and the more you need to be able to work on small pieces of the whole, because taking on the entire thing all at once becomes more and more impossible. This application cycle is going to be not only a test of the skills you've put together over your undergraduate career, but also a chance to practice the skills you will need to rely on more and more in grad school and in your career.

Budgeting Your Money

Applying to grad school comes with a lot of costs both obvious and hidden, but there are also some lesser-known ways that you can offset those costs if you plan ahead.

APPLICATION FEES

Almost every university you apply to will charge a fee that you must pay when you submit your application. You should plan on needing to pay such a fee to each university you apply to and, if you apply to more than one program in one university, a fee for each separate program. Fees vary by university, but given that they can range from $60 to $125 or more, you should budget about $100 per application while you are in the planning stages. As you research each school, you can plug in actual costs. You can offset this fee in some circumstances by applying for a fee waiver. If you are receiving a federal Pell Grant through financial aid, you will *probably* qualify for a fee waiver, but you will need to check with the separate universities on their individual policies. One thing to note about a fee waiver is that you can often submit the application for it *before* you submit your actual application. If that is the policy of the universities you are interested in, **you should apply right now**. I put that in bold because fee waivers can often be contingent on funding and, in many cases, they can be on a first come, first served basis. In other words, if the program spends its budget before you apply, you may not get the waiver. The second reason to apply early is that you want to give them enough time to approve your waiver before you send in your application. If you submit both at the same time, you may end up having to pay the fee out of pocket and then try to get reimbursed after you are approved. It's always easier to get approved first, then apply, than it is to get reimbursed after the fact. Make it a priority to find out if the universities you are applying to have a fee waiver, and apply now!

TRANSCRIPT FEES

Also plan to pay a fee to send transcripts from your current university to every university you are applying to. Some universities may request official transcripts only after you've been accepted, but most will require you to submit them along with your application. Fees can vary wildly from one university to another, from as low as $5 to $15 or more per transcript. Additionally, plan to request the transcripts at least three to four weeks before the due date of your application. If you wait until later, you may have to add a "rush" fee to the transcript cost.

Planning for this becomes even more important if you have attended more than one university in your college career. Remember when I told you that I attended three community colleges and two state universities as an undergrad? Well, you can imagine how much money I had to pay out-of-pocket to have transcripts sent from each of those schools to the grad programs I was applying to, not to mention the fact that this was before schools began doing this over the internet, so I was paying shipping fees on each of those. I spent a lot of money that I could have saved if I had planned ahead.

TESTING FEES

If the program you are applying to requires the Graduate Records Examinations test, or GRE, you will need to factor that into your budget as well. The current price of the GRE is $220, but you may need to pay more if the schools you are applying to require a particular subject test. As with the application fees, the GRE has an application you can fill out for a fee reduction. Unlike the fee waivers for application costs, this program will only reduce the fees, not eliminate them entirely. Also, as with the application fee waiver, if you know you need to take the GRE, you should apply for the fee reduction program *as soon as possible.*

You may not know the date you want to take the test yet or any of the other logistical details, but if you know you need the to take the test, apply for the fee reduction *right now.* The application is not automatic and will need to be processed. If you fill it out too close to the date of the test, you may not have enough time for the application to clear and you will have to pay out-of-pocket for the test fees. You will have a much easier time if you apply early than if you apply late and try to get reimbursed for fees you already paid.

HIDDEN COSTS

There are several other hidden costs to keep in mind while you are making your way through the process. I'm kind of taking for granted that you have access to a laptop or desktop computer. I really hate the idea that you will be trying to write essays or go through this application process on your phone. Good internet access is another thing I'm taking for granted here, but teaching in the Central Valley of California, I know that not all communities have access to stable internet service. If this means that you will need to spend extra time at your school or community library to access a decent computer or stable internet, you should budget in the time and cost associated with that.

If you need to take the GRE for one or more of your applications, you may need to include a time and money budget for GRE study. Often, college libraries will have GRE study materials available for checkout, but if you feel that you need to purchase material, or even pay for a GRE study class, those are additional costs to budget for. I cover GRE strategies later in the book, so be sure to look at those before you buy a book or pay for a course.

Because of the need to talk to professors during office hours, you may need to take additional trips to campus that aren't a part of your normal routine. That will mean extra time and gas money that you may not be expecting. Child care may be a hidden cost if you need to plan for additional child care in order to work on essays, meet with professors, or research programs.

Lastly, I want to emphasize again that this process will take a physical and emotional toll on you. I know that you are a badass who has conquered your undergrad program and who is about to graduate, but this process is a lot even for the most confident of students. The fact that you are submitting yourself to be judged by nameless, faceless strangers who hold your future in their hands is bound to cause some sleepless nights and a nervous stomach. Expect that you will need some self-care. If you're like me and your self-care involves coffee, chocolate, or even just quiet time on the couch, you'll need to plan to give yourself the time and budget for the expenses.

NEXT STEPS

Having considered many of the big-picture pieces of the application process, in the next few chapters we'll go into the materials you will need to prepare for your application package, starting with the personal statement. In my experience, this is the part that most often trips students up and causes delays. The solution is to make a plan, stick to it, and write! The next chapter will help guide you through the process.

8

THE PERSONAL STATEMENT

MORE THAN ANYWHERE ELSE in the application packet, your personal statement is *the* place where you will have a chance to tell the readers who you are and what you can do. So much of the application can be cold and driven by numbers or bullet points, but in the statement, we can show the sides of ourselves and our potential that we want to be seen. However, how to do this—how to write about yourself and how to know what it is a program even wants to hear—can be a complete mystery. This chapter is going to walk you through the process and give you a road map to writing a powerful statement that tells a story about you as a person and shows why you are going to be an amazing graduate student.

PROCRASTINATION

The personal statement is probably the most stressful part of this entire project. It's a huge guessing game about what exactly you are supposed to write about, what the committee readers might want to hear, and how personal it is supposed to get. Combine all those questions with just a general sense of fear and uncertainty, and the result is procrastination. Maybe it's different for you, but when I have doubts about how I am supposed to proceed with something, not to mention more general feelings of uncertainty, I am way less likely to dive into that project. I've noticed that many students respond in this way. The personal statement or statement of purpose is the thing they put off the most, and even when they sit down to tackle it, writing anything at all can feel like dragging the words out of their head one at a time. In this chapter, we'll go through everything you need to know about the statement, what it is, what messages you need to convey, and most importantly, how to start writing it.

None of this will take away the fear or the uncertainty completely, but the key here is to just start writing—writing anything! Once you get over the first hurdle of putting some words on a page, the next steps will be just slightly less daunting. So write, write, write.

PERSONAL STATEMENT, STATEMENT OF PURPOSE, OR LETTER OF INTENT?

Chances are, if you are applying to multiple programs, you will find requests for one or more of the following among the application instructions: a personal statement, a statement of purpose, or a letter of intent. Basically, each of these documents conveys the same information, but in somewhat different ways. The big picture is that the people who will read these statements want to know whether you have the academic skills you will need to do well in the program's required classes, whether you have the personal qualities that will make you good at the job or career you are training for, and, if it's a PhD program, whether you have research projects and interests that will be a good fit for the department and that will make a solid dissertation subject.

If the department you are applying to asks for either a personal statement or a statement of purpose, they are probably looking for answers to all those questions in one document. They want a roughly two- to three-page essay that covers these questions and introduces you to the readers on the committee. If they request both a personal statement and a separate statement of purpose, they are basically asking you to split out the personal and professional sides of the questions into two documents. In my experience, it is more common to find PhD programs asking for separate personal statements and statements of purpose, because they want you to go into more depth about the type of research you want to do in their program and your general research interests. Their application instructions should give you some clues about how they want you to split these things out.

No matter what they call the document they are requesting—statement of purpose, personal statement, or letter of intent—they all want to know basically the same things (the question is, how much space are they giving you to write all of it?). And again, if they want two separate documents, they are usually asking you to write about your academic qualifications in one and your personal qualifications in the other.

What Do They Want to Know?

Any department you are applying to basically wants answers to the following questions:

1. Can you do the academic work you will be asked to do as part of the program? (Academic qualifications)
2. Are you likely to be good at doing the job the program is training people for? (Personal and professional qualifications)
3. Are you going to make their life difficult? (Red flags)

ACADEMIC WORK You are applying to an academic program that will ask you to do rigorous academic work at a graduate level. Don't let that wording scare you. Graduate-level work isn't all that different from the work you were doing in your upper-division classes in your major as an undergraduate. It's more concentrated on particular subjects or skills, but it doesn't require you to suddenly be a genius. The most important skill you can bring with you into graduate school is your ability to learn, to know how to learn, and if you have earned a bachelor's degree, you have already had to practice this a lot. The program you are applying to wants to know what evidence you have that you can learn and that you will perform well, at least well enough to finish.

PERSONAL AND PROFESSIONAL QUALITIES For many of the programs you will be applying to, the degree program constitutes basic training for a particular career that you are interested in going into once you graduate. Teacher, social worker, counselor, engineer—each of these careers requires you to go through a specialty graduate program that will give you a baseline set of skills and training to do the job. But having that training is only one part of being good at any job. In many careers, your personality and your background are going to play a large role in how well you perform professionally. Programs want to know that you have a set of personality traits that pair well with the job you are training for. This can be a little tricky, so have conversations with your team members to help you think through the types of traits the admission committee likely wants to see. If you are going into teaching, for instance, it will be key to show your capacity for patience, your ability to communicate, and your skill in working with students in the relevant age ranges. If you're going into training to be a counselor, it will be important to show your capacity for empathy in your essay.

The focus will be a little different for programs that are largely academic. If you are entering a PhD program in sociology or psychology, for example, a majority of what you will be training for is probably to do research and eventually become a research professor. In this case, you may want to showcase your dedication to the subject matter and research itself. You can talk about the parts of your personality that will make you a careful and insightful researcher. Sometimes, those qualities may overlap with the traits mentioned above. A strong sense of empathy may be a great trait for a sociologist looking to understand different aspects of social life, whereas empathy may be less important than meticulous attention to detail if you are applying to a PhD program in mathematics.

MAKING THEIR LIFE HARDER This last one may sound silly, but it's truer than you might think. Professors are often overworked and stressed, and they have a keen sense for students or situations that are likely to take a lot of extra time or work. The more that you can do in your materials to reassure them that you are a sure bet to do well in your classes, produce high-quality research, and generally not cause them headaches, the better your chances are. If, on the other hand, you spend time complaining about your current department, seem combative about your theoretical or research goals, or come off as entitled, the people reading your essay will have those clues to go on in assessing you as a potential student (or problem).

Luckily, in my years working with so many first-generation students, this hasn't been an issue for most. If anything, you all are too reluctant to brag about yourselves and what you are capable of, rather than being over-the-top in praise of your own genius or unable to read the room. But striking the right tone in telling strangers about who you are can be tricky, and you'll need outside readers (your team members) to help make sure your statement conveys an accurate and winning impression.

HOW TO APPROACH WRITING

My approach to writing these documents is basically that stories are much easier to remember than lists. Given that the members of an admission committee can be asked to go through hundreds of applications, you need to do everything you can to keep your application from becoming just another document on their computer screens, and to keep your story in their heads after they are done reading your essays. In my opinion, you can have the most impressive credentials in the world, but after a few hours of reading applications, the numbers and the awards and the internships all start to blur together. However, a good personal story is something that will be completely unique to your application. No one else will be able to write about the experiences you've had or copy your unique voice. Talking about personal moments, unique to your own background, will help your essay stand out in ways that other essays that are focused on lists of accomplishments will lack.

What I mean by *stories* are pieces of writing that tell the reader something about who you are and the qualities and traits you bring to the table, but that are told in a narrative format rather than a list of personal qualities—for instance, talking about your motivations for going to grad school and a personal incident or event that sparked your interest in the field. Maybe you are interested in becoming a psychologist because you had a therapist who made a huge impact on you at an important time in your life or were especially inspired by a high school counselor. The idea is to tell the readers something more about yourself through unique stories rather than just listing qualities you claim to possess.

There are a few reasons why I think stories are a good idea, given that applications always ask you to describe yourself. If we simply make a list of rather abstract traits and qualities, how will the reader distinguish our self-description from those of the other applicants? Say that you and I are applying to the same program in counseling. In our statements of purpose, we each might write that we are "caring and empathetic."

That's easy enough for anyone to say, whether it's true or not. I could be a horribly judgmental person, mostly selfish and unconcerned with other people, but that isn't going to stop me from describing myself as caring and empathetic. What kind of weight will such vague phrases carry with the readers? Through stories, we can *show* the readers our wonderful qualities and traits in action, rather than just *telling* them we have these attributes. I may be able to *say* I'm caring, but if you have stories about your work with family, friends, and the community that demonstrate *how* you care and your commitment to working with others, your description of yourself as caring and empathetic is going to be much more believable than my bland phrases.

Another reason I really favor stories is that for the readers, every application is just a file on a computer screen. Readers know, intellectually, that there is a real, living person on the other side of the document they are reading, but after a few applications that reality starts to get lost and the digital pages start to blur together. At least when a professor is reading your papers or grading a test, they can attach a name and a face to what they are reading. They likely remember your contributions in class. But the readers on an admission committee have none of that background or personal experience with you, and so, for all intents and purposes, you are easily reduced to a name and a computer file. Stories are a way for us to push back against that, to make ourselves come across as human and relatable to the people reading our essays. When the admission committee is often reading a hundred or more applications, anything we can do to stand out from the crowd in a positive way is worth the effort.

Start by Writing Stories, Not Essays

Time and time again, the biggest issue I see students face in producing the personal statement is simply starting the writing process. So, here's my biggest piece of advice: Just start writing. That sounds dumb, but let me tell you what I mean:

- Don't start by trying to have an entire essay mapped out in your head before putting words to paper. That strategy usually only leads to procrastination, because we rarely get to a point where the essay in our head feels ready to start writing.
- Don't start at the beginning; start in the middle. One thing that trips people up all the time is not knowing how to start a piece. If you are struggling on how to start an essay, skip the beginning altogether and write a part of the essay you feel more comfortable with. There's no rule that you have to write your first draft from beginning to end.
- Start writing stories before you start writing essays. If you are getting hung up on what you need to write for an essay, start by writing stories instead. Write a story about a time when you realized that this career field was what you wanted to do. Write about a time when you did a similar type of work and the impact it had on you. Don't worry that you aren't sure if it fits in your larger essay structure, just write. We'll figure the essay part out later.

If you are having trouble thinking what to write about, start instead by thinking about the career you are training to go into. What makes a good *[insert career here]*? What traits make a good teacher? What personal qualities make a good researcher or counselor or psychologist? Make a list of the qualities you most associate with the position, aiming for a few key words or phrases. These are the central traits to convey in the stories you tell. If empathy and understanding are a big part of the career you want to go into, they should be a big part of what you write your stories about. Use this list of traits to help you think about personal experiences that can become relevant stories.

After you have drafted a few brief stories about yourself, highlighting the qualities you bring to the table and the skills you possess, take this set of stories to a team member or two. And don't wait—bring in team members to read your work early and often. We can get hung up easily if we are worried that we need to present only our best, most finished work to our team. The issue is that we are often not the best judge of what parts of our story are the most compelling or relevant. Because we experienced it ourselves, in telling the story we can sometimes get caught up in the details, trying to depict what happened accurately. Good team members won't mind if you ask to run a first draft by them, as long as you tell them exactly what it is and what specific input would be helpful. Let them know that you are trying to find a central theme or story for your essay, and these stories are what you have so far. Brainstorm with them about which stories should be taken out and which should be given a big role in the final essay. Hopefully, these conversations will help you identify a strong story-based theme for your essay, and you can start to map out a structure for your statement, deciding what to use and what to leave out.

Writing for a Reason

After you have some raw material for your essay, it's time to start molding it into an actual essay. The first thing to keep in mind is the thesis statement: that you are an awesome student who is going to be amazing in this new program and go on to be a world-class professional in your chosen field. That's the big idea, and it's what every section in the essay needs to point to, in one way or another. I say this because, when we are writing about ourselves and our experiences, it can be easy to get caught up in details that don't matter or in trying to explain aspects of our record that we aren't confident about. Both of those detract from the bigger point of the essay. It can be easy to spend a lot of words on details that were important in the moment but that may not be necessary in getting your point across. Remember, your personal statement is not a biography. You don't owe the readers "the truth, the whole truth, and nothing but the truth." Instead, you owe them a true version

PERSONAL STATEMENT PROMPTS

1. Tell a story about a time you overcame something difficult and how that relates to a quality or trait that will help you in grad school.
2. Tell a story about a time you failed or fell short, what you learned from it, and how that will help you in your grad program.
3. Tell a story about a challenging class you had and how you dealt with it to pass the class. What did this experience give you that will help you with grad school?
4. Tell a story about how you came to realize what you want to study and what draws you to the career field you've picked. How does this experience help give you tools you need to do well in grad school?
5. Tell a story about a time someone in your life helped you in a way that is like the type of work you want to do in the future (e.g., nursing, social work, psychology). How did that experience shape you, and how will that make you a better student and more successful in your future career?
6. Tell a story about how your own experiences will help you relate to the people you hope to work with in your career, and how this will make you a better professional.
7. Tell a story about what inspired your research in your focal area. How will that inspiration help make you a better grad student or professional?
8. Tell a story about a particular person you knew who made an impact on you. How did that individual help or inspire you, and how will that experience help make you a more effective grad student or professional?
9. Tell a story about a time you've done work that was similar to what you want to do in the future (e.g., research, social work, counseling). What were the circumstances, and what did you learn? How will this help make you a better grad student or professional?
10. Tell a story about how you've grown during your time in college and how that growth will help you in your new program and as a professional.
11. Tell a story about something unique about you and who you are or something unique that you've experienced. How will those unique traits or experiences make you a better grad student or professional?

of events, told in a way that highlights the best of your personal and professional attributes. That may mean leaving out parts of your biography, or some events in the timeline of a story, but remember that the whole point of including the story in this essay is that it led to your interests and success as a student or will help you be a terrific professional. Everything you are putting on the page should be in service to that one conclusion—you belong in this program.

Best Practices and Writing Techniques

Your personal statement is a road map for your application as a whole. It introduces you to the readers and walks them through your personal, professional, and academic qualifications. To do that, the essay must include markers and guides along the way, a kind of repeated checking-in to make sure the readers know where they are in the essay, where it is heading, and why they are reading it. This may sound a little strange or excessive for a relatively short document, but one thing I've found is that we easily get lost in telling a story and forget that the story is supposed to be telling the reader something specific about us and our capabilities. We need to make sure that we are reminding the reader of those things at each step of the way. In practical terms, what I'm suggesting comes down to a few concrete practices. In the introduction, make sure that toward the end of the first paragraph, you remind the reader of the major topics that you are going to cover over the course of your essay and how those topics tie back to your bigger thesis—which is, don't forget, "I am awesome and I belong in your program!"

For example, over the course of the essay, you may be planning on talking about your motivation in going into the field, your volunteer experiences, and your academic qualifications. Your opening paragraph should provide a sort of a road map that sets up those topics in the order you are going to talk about them, ending on your thesis message. So, something like this: "My history of involvement with care work, coupled with my volunteer experiences and my strong academic performance, including a 3.5 GPA in my upper-division psychology courses, makes me an excellent candidate for your program." This sentence alerts the reader that you are going to talk about your involvement in care work, tying this to your academic and professional motivations. It also puts a big highlight of your application front and center, so they see it right away. GPA doesn't have to be the big highlight—it could be your experience, your motivation, or even personal traits that make you well qualified. The point is that you need to hit the highlights *early* to focus the reader's mind on their importance to the route and the destination.

Now, follow this road map in organizing and writing the rest of the essay. Cover the topics you mentioned at the end of the introduction, in the same order in which you brought them up. When you start a paragraph on a new topic, make sure that the opening and closing sentences continue to provide a road map for the readers, who should never lose sight of why what they are reading is important to know about you and how it supports your thesis. In a paragraph about your academic experience, you might start with something like this: "My academic background in psychology gives me a strong base to enter your program," going from there into your history and experiences. Then, at the end, make sure you hit them with it again: "Finishing a bachelor's degree in psychology has been enormously challenging, but the skill sets I've gained over that time will be extremely useful when I take the *** and *** courses that are required in your program." You should absolutely adapt these sentences to match your own writing style and tone, but the big idea is there. You need to keep the big picture front and center throughout your essay, so that all the information you're giving them points to your thesis: "I am awesome and I belong in your program!"

Writing About Academic Experience

The first task in writing about the skills you've developed is recognizing those skills to begin with. Too many students downplay their academic credentials and the skills they bring with them from their undergraduate education. The theme is that they thought college was going to be harder, or that the lower-division classes were easier than the upper-division classes in their major, or that courses were harder at their community college before they transferred. That may be the case, but there are other reasons why things seem this way. For one, you aren't necessarily aware of all the ways you've grown and matured that have made passing classes easier. By the time you're close to graduating, you've had to do a ton of writing, analysis, tests, and projects. In your first few years, those things were all relatively new for most people and so seemed a lot tougher. Second, you've most likely had to develop a time schedule and task organization habits that you didn't have before. Many of us come in being able to write an essay the night before it's due and keep that habit until it stops working at some point in our college career. If that's the case, you've had to develop a lot of skills that help you take on larger projects, multiple due dates, and more demanding essays.

Okay, the pep talk was nice, but what do you write about when it comes to your academic experience? First, let's talk skills. Things to do to get you started: List out all the upper-division classes you took. For each class, write down at least three skills you needed to pass that class. Writing, math, analysis, project management, statistics, public speaking, team exercises, and so on. Then list out the major themes you went over in each class. What big-picture things did you talk about in the class? If you're having trouble, try to find a copy of the syllabus for the class to refresh your memory. If you can, use your memory or your syllabus to list out any major projects or papers you had to do and the tasks you had to perform to complete them.

The goal is to try and match the skills that you've developed over these courses to skills that are needed for the program you are applying to. Every program requires writing and analysis, so talk about the classes you took that helped prepare you to do this in their program. What projects or papers did you finish that helped you practice writing and analysis? What types of class discussions did you participate in, or what theories did you explore, that expanded your ability to break down complicated ideas and explain them in writing? If you did stats or math, what classes did you take and what skills did you need to pass those classes?

You need to give the readers all this information in a way that is not just a list of skills. Tell them about what you learned in your classes, but pivot to how those skills relate to what you will be doing in their classes. If you aren't sure what classes you will be taking, look through the "Grad Handbooks" section of chapter 6 again and pick out a couple of classes you will be taking in the first year. Most of the time, the skills you will need to do well in those classes should stand out. Be sure to mention by name a class or two that you're looking forward to taking. For example, "In my sociological theory class, we had extended discussions about theorists like Karl Marx and Émile Durkheim. We had to break down complicated ideas that were presented to us in the reading and apply them to current events and situations in our own lives. The reading and writing were a challenge, but I believe that it prepared me well for the class in theories of education that students in your program take in the first semester." This gets across some of the skills that you bring with you, and it shows that you've done your homework about their program. Most applicants don't mention anything specific about the program they are applying to. If you do, your application will automatically stand out.

Remember . . .

Talking about skills you learned in a class is not the same as saying that you are an *expert* in those skills. A lot of us only passed statistics or math classes with our fingers crossed and a candle lit to help us through, and because of that a lot of students feel uncomfortable putting these classes and skills on their CV or their personal statement. The idea here is not that you are going to remember every aspect of your stats class, or every formula from your math course. What you are saying is that when you were put in a position to need to learn these skills, you succeeded, and you can do that again. You have the capacity to take on a stats class, a math class, or a bio class, and even though you may not come out of it a stats or bio genius, you can do what it takes to pass that class. Once you get into a program, you will be taking a lot of new classes. No one expects that you will walk in the door being an expert on everything you learned as an undergrad, but what you *are* telling them is that you know how to learn, and you will be bringing this skill with you to their program.

WHAT COUNTS AS EXPERIENCE?

There are several master's programs that ask you to have some forms of experience in a field related to the one you are applying to. For instance, master of social work programs will sometimes ask applicants to have two hundred hours of experience in a care work field. Often, this requirement will scare off potential applicants who don't already work in the field or who haven't had formal internships in a relevant area. However, this requirement is often not as clear-cut as it may seem at first.

Right up front, you need to make sure you are paying careful attention to the language of the application instructions. If the instructions state that you have to have a certain number of years of employment in a particular field and a letter from a supervisor, then okay, not too much wiggle room there. But if the application uses language that is a little more vague about the experience they want, such as requiring two hundred hours of "related experience," you can make an argument in your application about the things that you've done that count as experience. For most programs, what counts are experiences that are directly related to the field you are interested in studying and working in, but those experiences do not necessarily have to be "work" experiences or internships. Being employed or having an internship can be one great way of showing you have experience, but it isn't necessarily the only way you can show your experience.

Just as with your letters of recommendation, you need to consider exactly what it is you are applying to study and what it is you will do with the degree. The programs you are applying to want to see that you have experiences that are relevant to both those aspects. If you are applying to a PhD program in sociology, they will want to see experiences that are relevant to that program, such as social science research experience coupled with a solid understanding of sociology as a discipline and a theoretical perspective. Given that sociology covers a broad range of human experiences, your own personal experiences with things like poverty, inequality, race, gender, and other major areas that sociology studies can be extremely relevant. If you can show that your personal experiences are going to help make you good at the things you will need to do in graduate school and later as a professor, then those experiences are directly relevant even if they didn't result in research papers. For a field more directly related to a job outside academia, like a teaching credential, experience can come in different forms, like your experiences working with siblings, babysitting, or being a summer camp counselor.

The goal is to show your background in the types of situations that are relevant to the job you will be training for. From that perspective, experience can be things that you've gone through, not necessarily things that you've done yourself. For instance, having a good counselor who was able to help with a difficult time, or a social worker who helped you or your family, is a type of experience that you can draw on in your applications. Being able to show that you understand why this particular career is so valuable because of your own background can be an important way to demonstrate that you understand the career you are choosing for yourself, and that your experiences have shaped your motivations to go into that field. Even having had a bad teacher, counselor, or social worker could be considered a type of experience if you can use it to show how that person shaped your outlook on the career and how you want to do the job in a different way. The point that we are looking to make is that we have exposure to the field we want to go into and that we have an idea of the importance of that field and what it can mean for others if we do it right. Being able to show this goes a long way toward convincing a reader that you are a good fit for a program or a career field.

Self-Doubt

One aspect of being a first-generation college student is that we tend to discount our achievements and our background, seeing them as not measuring up or not being relevant to the goals we have. This is a tendency that you will need to start pushing back on. A big part of the process of applying to graduate school, or applying for a future job, is to convince them that your experiences and your background are directly relevant. You will have a hard time doing that if you can't convince even yourself! This is another time when a good team can be important. Sit down with someone from your team that you trust, and talk with them about your background. Don't trust your own intuition if it's telling you that nothing you've gone through is important to what you want to do. Instead, talk with another person who can help you think about the ways in which the things you've done in the past apply to the things you want to do in the future.

MASTER'S ESSAY STRUCTURE

Intro and Personal Story

I am a big fan of starting with a personal story that gives the reader a vivid idea of who you are and why you are interested in the field. The readers are going to see a million essays that start with "I am a . . . who has . . . and wants to . . ." or "As far back as I can remember, I have wanted to be a . . . ." This sort of essay opening is so commonplace that it will only help your essay get lost in the shuffle. Instead, look at your list of stories and see if there is one that really stands out as being evocative, emotional, or just a strong representation of who you are. Look back at the list of qualities we talked about earlier and think about which of those you want to emphasize the most and choose the story that will be best at demonstrating them.

Personal Experience

In this section, talk about the qualities you have that will make you excellent at being a graduate student and excellent at being a professional in the field. See if you can identify a good story to organize this section around that highlights some of these traits and make sure to really hammer home what you bring to the table.

Academic Experience

This is the place to center your stories on your academic strengths and personal connections to the field. Be sure to hit all the highlights of your academic background here. Don't be shy—you need to sound prepared and awesome.

Why This Program?

One thing that the people reading your essay will love is for you to write about *them*. I know that sounds weird, but it's completely true. A couple of years ago, I was working on a hiring committee for our department. We had to read about fifty applications, including multiple statements, CVs, letters, and more. It got boring quickly, because a lot of them started to sound the same, and it was apparent when someone had written what amounted to an all-purpose "letter of interest," just changing the school's name and sending the same document out with each of their applications. Applying for jobs is a lot like applying for grad programs: It can be a numbers game, so I don't fault applicants for using a single set of materials for their applications, but if I can easily tell that's what they are doing, it makes me wonder if they have any idea about the place they are applying to or any genuine interest. Once, I came across an application that mentioned a colleague of mine by name. It was as if a little jolt of electricity went through me and shook me out of my boredom. Here was something specific, about someone I knew. The applicant also included other details about our department, like the classes we offer and why they were interested in teaching some of our specific courses (though they lost points because they didn't mention *me* by name—just kidding). The fact that this person had taken the time to research our school and our department made a big impression.

You can do this too. Toward the end of your essay, you should have a section that goes into specifics about the program you are applying to and what makes it a good fit for what you want to do—summing up why you are a good fit for this department. Again, draw on the list of classes you gleaned from the grad handbook or website. What classes do they offer that sound really interesting to you? Are there certain sequences of courses that perfectly fit your area of interest? Is there anything about the way the program is organized that is different from other programs you've researched, like a focus they have on a particular area, how they split up classes, when they offer classes, or even things they list as core values on their mission statement. Any of those can be great to point out when explaining why you are interested in joining the program. You can also find the bio pages of faculty members and see if any research interests of theirs match your interests and passions. For instance, you might say something like "I am excited that your program offers classes on gerontology and working with elderly populations.

One of my areas of interest in being a social worker is to work in hospice care, or in other capacities with older clients. I'm glad your program has a focus on this area and it made your program stand out as a great fit for me." Or "Professor *X*'s research on *Y* was really interesting to me since my undergraduate classes focused a lot on *Y* and I would be excited to learn more." Anything that shows you have done research about the program and know some specific details is a good idea.

Goals and Conclusion

The last section should finish strongly with your main message of the entire essay, *I'm awesome and I will be awesome in your program*. Here is a great place to talk about your goals, things you want to do once you finish the program, areas you may want to specialize in for your career, and how earning this degree will be a win for you, but also for the communities you want to serve. Go back over your major points—you're awesome, you've done awesome stuff in your life and in school, and they would be crazy not to let you in.

WHAT SHOULD YOU WRITE ABOUT—AND HOW PERSONAL SHOULD YOU GET?

Special Note: Writing About Trauma

This is a tough one. Something that comes up a lot in reading hundreds of personal statements over the years is that we often approach the essay as a type of biography. It makes sense—it's literally called a personal statement, so they must want us to get personal and tell them our story. Being a first-generation student often means that we were raised in rough circumstances and that we had to overcome a lot to get where we are. I've seen or heard about students who experienced abuse, homelessness, deportation, or persecution—almost any hardship you can imagine. I'm constantly amazed at the things that people have had to endure—and that they have managed to overcome everything and finish their college education.

I've also seen students who are reluctant to write the personal statement because they feel that they are *required* to write about their background and their trauma, which can be immensely triggering for some people. For others, the reluctance comes from the fact that they just don't want to share aspects of themselves with strangers, and since they feel that this is required for the personal statement, they hesitate to start writing.

Let me state this clearly: *You do not owe anyone anything, you don't owe the school you are applying to your story or your trauma, you do not have to reveal anything you don't want to, and you are not required to elicit sympathy to be accepted*. You owe the admission committee one thing: an application that portrays you in the best possible light and makes the best possible case for why you should be admitted. You have a ton of positive things going for you that have nothing to do with what you have experienced in the past, so if you don't want to talk about something or there is a part of your life you don't want to go into, *you do not have to.*

The goal here is to showcase you, your talents, your skills, and your potential. Everything you include in the essay should contribute to reaching that goal. That said, you don't have to avoid any or all of the negatives or challenges in your past. If perseverance is a particular quality that you want to demonstrate to the admission committee, talking about a moment in life when you had to overcome something difficult could help you make the case. If you want to argue that you will be able to relate directly to the people you will be serving in the future as a counselor or a social worker, talking about the issues you've faced that will help you relate to people in tough situations can be a good way to do this. The point here is to be less concerned with *what* you are sharing in your essay, and more concerned with *why* you are sharing it.

If you were writing a comprehensive biography about yourself, you would need to give a full and complete story of what has happened to you. However, for the purposes of this essay, what happened to you is less important than explaining why the experiences you've chosen to share make you an excellent candidate for the program you are applying to. Let me give you an example from my life and my own personal statement.

I grew up poor. Not as poor as many people, but poor enough that I have early memories of food stamps and government cheese. My parents had stories of bullet casings being found in the shag carpeting of their first apartment and someone sneaking through a bedroom window to steal my father's wedding ring. Some of those experiences really shaped me and the way I view the world. When I first wrote a personal statement for applications to sociology PhD programs, I talked about those childhood memories. I shared about my dad being a truck driver and my mom staying home and educating us. When I read that essay now, I realize that I shared a lot of things that had a deep impact on who I am, but I never made the case for why those experiences would help make me a good sociological researcher, or why my background would help me finish the program I was applying to. I remember thinking that this was a place to talk about who I was, but I was unsure what the readers would want to know. Given that I also had a chip on my shoulder about who I was and where I was from, I wasn't about to pretend I was some fancy asshole who went to an Ivy League school. Talking about my background was my own way of staying true to myself, but what I didn't realize was that there were ways I could do that *and* tell the readers *why* that background would help make me an excellent sociologist.

My point here is that if you want to talk about something painful or difficult from your past, you are absolutely entitled to. However, the big question about anything you might put in this essay is its relevance to the purpose and the thesis, and whether that connection will be clear to the readers. Your *why* should always be some variation of the same message: "This experience, skill, or trait makes me an awesome candidate to do well in your program and to go on to do well in the job you are training me for." Writing about poverty, experiencing a painful personal episode, or dealing with a setback can all be powerful ways to show your resilience, your ability to overcome obstacles, or your ability to persevere in the face of adversity. These are traits that all graduate students need. If you decide that you *want* to share a painful story, be sure to remind the readers that you are telling them this because of what it says *about* you, not simply because it *happened* to you. The person that came through to the other side of that rough experience is the person they will be getting in their program, someone who overcame something major and is still ready to take on the world.

Experiencing a Thing Versus Writing About a Thing: Why Your First Draft Will Always Seem Corny

Writing a personal statement is a kind of trick. You are writing about something you lived through, a real moment in your life, and capturing everything that happened in that moment can be hard. But you don't need to capture *everything* that happened. Telling a story has a lot to do with what you leave out, as well as what you put in. Since you were the person who experienced this moment, you have access to a lot of detail that played an important role, but writing about a thing is different than experiencing a thing. The writing of a thing is a trick, it's a skill, and it's probably not a skill you've practiced a lot. Because of that, when you go to write about an important moment in your life, your first draft will probably sound cheesy or just feel hollow when you read it and compare it to a detailed and emotional memory.

You have to let your first draft sound cheesy. You must get it into your head now that your first draft will not really capture your experience in the way that you want it to, and you have to trust your team to help you revise your draft in ways that will move you in the right direction. The problem for a lot of people is that they get frustrated and disheartened when they write about something important, and it comes out sounding flat. In some ways, it can cheapen the memory of that important thing that happened to you. At one point, I tried to write about my dad dying when I was in my mid-twenties. It's a memory that is powerful enough to still overwhelm me twenty years later, but when I write about it, I can't ever capture or even come close to getting across how that moment felt. When I reread the things I wrote, they seem to make the momentous thing I lived through seem small and mundane. It hurt too much to keep trying and I had to stop.

Writing about a thing is having to relive it, and if an experience was especially awful, no one wants to relive it any more than they absolutely have to. Writing your personal statement will be a process in having to confront some powerful memories and capture them in a way that does them justice. But writing about a thing is different than living a thing. The writing is a trick, it's a skill, it's something you must practice before it will come out sounding good. Trust that your team will not let you send out something that sounds off. Give them time to go through drafts of your work and be prepared to write and rewrite about something until it sounds the way it felt. That process is not something that can be done in one draft—it will take time and commitment.

If You Don't Talk About It, It Doesn't Exist

As you make your way through drafts of your statement, remember that as far as your readers are concerned, if it's not in the statement of purpose, then for all intents and purposes it doesn't exist. What I mean by this is that, while most admission committee members will take their time and look through your application materials carefully and consider them all, the reality is that we can't *count on* the members doing that. Practically speaking, this means that if there is something that you want the committee to know, some bright spot on your record, some amazing thing about you, or what you've done, *it needs to be in this statement*. I've run into a situation repeatedly when working with students: I read the statement draft they send me, I'm puzzled because I've had them in class, I look up their academic record, and I find out they have an amazing GPA that *they never even mentioned in their statement*. Or I'll know from conversations that they spent time doing an internship or volunteering with an organization, experiences that never come up in the statement they give me.

You can't rely on the readers building a story about you from the various documents you submit; rather, you need to prepackage and hand them that story in your statement. If you have a great GPA but never mention it, there is a chance that the reader won't know about it. If you've been on the dean's list, received an award, or had a relevant experience, you need to talk about that in the statement. A frequent justification I get from students for leaving things out is that the information is in other places in the application, such as the CV or the transcripts. The reality is that the statement is the one place where we should be summarizing *all* of the information for the reader and giving it the context and meaning that we want it to carry. When in doubt, *put it in*. Then give the draft to your team members and let them give you feedback about whether a certain item needs to be a part of the overall essay or not.

Why Good Grades Are Not Enough

We've already talked about what to do if your grades are not as high as you think they should be. It's true that no one is ever satisfied with their grades, no matter how high. At the same time, I've worked with students who are convinced that because of their stellar GPA, they will have an easy time getting into a good program. It is true that an impressive GPA is a great trophy to put on prominent display throughout your application, hammering home to the reader that you have a track record of not only passing classes but excelling in them. But that doesn't mean you should rely on your GPA to tell your whole story for you, as if that number somehow relays to the readers everything important. Such a strategy will not be as successful as you might think, even if you have an outstanding GPA.

Think about this essay and application from the perspective of the reader. A high GPA is obviously awesome, and it definitely tells the reader that this student has worked hard and achieved something special. But a high GPA, in itself, cannot answer all the important questions the reader will have. Focusing on GPA as your major selling point sometimes means that you neglect to talk about your experiences outside of the classroom and can often come across as valuing a number you earned more than what you learned. A good grade tells the reader that you performed well in a class, but it doesn't tell them what you learned in that class, what it meant to you, or how you will apply that learning to what you will do in the program.

If you do count on your GPA to tell your whole story, it can be disheartening if you don't get accepted your first time around. It can feel like there is nothing left to add to your package—after all, your GPA is top notch, and isn't that the most important thing? The reality is that there is a whole lot more to you than your GPA. While grades are obviously important, presenting yourself as a well-rounded person, sharing relevant experiences, and making sure that your stories give the reader key information about you in a memorable way can outshine even the GPA.

Final Thoughts on Your Story and Your Essay

The application process can be extremely impersonal. You're asked to write up huge sections of your life as numbers and bullet points. It can feel like all your effort, growth, and potential has been boiled down to a single number. I remember going through the process feeling completely inadequate because I didn't have a single scholarship, publication, award, or accolade to put on my application. I think the best I could do was note the fact that I was on the dean's list once or twice. When we go through this process, it's natural for our brain to highlight all the things we *don't* have. It's much easier to see the things we are lacking than to be positive and remind ourselves of the things we have accomplished. As a first-generation student, don't forget to remind yourself throughout this process that at one point in your life, graduating college seemed like an entirely remote and hypothetical situation. Many of us came from high schools where dropping out might have seemed just as likely as going to college. My wife was one of the first people in her extended family to graduate from high school, so the thought of graduating college was something that barely registered on the horizon for her. I mention this because it can be easy to forget how far we've come to reach where we are now. Your accomplishments matter, even if they didn't come with a trophy, a scholarship, or a certificate. You have to be your own best cheerleader in this project. If you write about the things you've done with enthusiasm and pride, the readers on the admission committee will be influenced to use those same perceptions to view what you are showing them. But if you are timid and apologetic about the things you've accomplished, well, the readers will pick up on that too. This is the time and place to be bold and to work on seeing the best in yourself and what you are capable of. Practicing this now will help you develop another skill that will pay off in the future.

SPECIAL INSTRUCTIONS FOR PhD STATEMENTS

Research Statements

The templates and instructions that we've gone through in this chapter can broadly apply to either a master's application, a credential application, or a PhD application, but there are some differences in a PhD application that you should be alert to. The overall goals of the PhD statement are those we've covered in this chapter, with the overarching theme that you are an awesome applicant who will do amazing things in the PhD program and go on to do amazing things as a professional. However, a PhD application may include a few elements that are different from applications to other program types. For example, PhD programs often request a personal statement *and* a statement of purpose or research statement. The personal statement is pretty much along the lines outlined above: You'll want to describe your personal, professional, and academic qualifications for the program, talk about your motivations and background, and relate your experiences to the program. What is different is that PhD programs are often highly focused on graduate students producing their own research or being a part of a research team or laboratory, so they will also want to know what types of research you are interested in doing and what areas of study you want to focus on. These are the questions your statement of purpose or research statement should address. While the content of this separate statement is a little different from that of the personal statement, the principal idea that you want to get across is the same: "I'm an awesome student who will do well in your academic program and go on to be an amazing professional in the field." That is the thesis statement that all the information you cover in your statement of purpose or research statement should point back to. Let's cover some of the specific things you'll want to go over in this statement.

Research Skills

A PhD program will be centered, first and foremost, on you becoming an expert in a particular field and performing research in the field in the course of your studies. Your statement of purpose should therefore be focused on demonstrating to the reader that you have the personal, professional, and academic background necessary to perform well in their program and to do the type of research that will be required. You can highlight this in several ways, but you'll want to specifically talk about the classes you've taken and the skills you've developed as part of your undergraduate program. Again, look at the courses the program will require you to take as part of your first two years. Most of the time, these will include methods and theory courses, whose syllabi can give you a good idea of the types of skills you should be highlighting for the readers. You can talk about papers you wrote for related undergraduate courses, special techniques and methodologies you studied, and topics you covered. The point is to make the case that you have some background experience in the tools and techniques you will be learning, not that you are already an expert.

Research Topics

In addition to the skills you will need for doing research, talk about the kind of research you want to do and the areas you want to study. The big picture here is that PhD programs are often a long and involved process of gaining expertise in a particular field. The program that you are applying to will want to make sure that they have appropriate faculty members to pair you with during your time there. If you are super-interested in studying cell biology, but the program you are applying to doesn't have someone on the faculty who specializes in that area, then there won't be anyone for you to work closely with, and the program might not be a good fit. You don't usually have to be extremely specific about the minute details of an area you want to go into, but you should clearly identify the general topics you want to study and the methods you might use.

Who You Can Work With

This is another big area that you should touch on. Knowing the topics that you are interested in studying, look through the department's web page and identify professors that might be a good fit to work with. Mention at least three professors in the department and talk about what areas of their research fit well with your topics of interest. You don't need to read everything the professors have written, of course, but it would be a good idea to read their faculty profile page, see what they've been working on recently and what they've published in the past few years, and bring up some of that in this statement. For example, you could write something like this: "My interest in the politics of land distribution in the United States in the early 1800s would fit well with the work that Dr. Stevens has done recently on land grants and political parties." Again, you don't have to be super-specific, but give the readers a general sense of how your interests might fit with the professors you mention and the work they do.

NEXT STEPS

The next piece of the application packet is the CV, a specific type of résumé that you can use to reinforce the points you've made in your statement. In the next chapter, we'll go over what to put in your CV, how to present the material, and how to best use the CV to make your experiences shine.

PERSONAL STATEMENT EXAMPLES

Let's go through some real examples of personal statements that I've worked on with students. The point is to highlight the areas that we changed and how the changes helped to develop the essay and the story that the student was telling.

The following is an intro I received from a student in their first draft. Read through it and take some notes on how the statement sounds, what comes across about the student, and the impression that it makes.

> Growing up in a nearby rural town, I did not have much exposure to larger-scale issues, nor did I understand the social injustice that individuals were experiencing. Living in such a small town can lead to conformity, ignorance, and depression. I am a byproduct of the small-town mindset. Upon graduating high school, I did not have the desire to pursue higher education and only attended the local community college to please my parents. My parents had higher expectations for me because I had been a stellar student since elementary—but I had lost my drive and determination. Soon after, I flunked out of community college and decided to work minimum-wage jobs because they at least paid the bills. Like most of my classmates, I settled with staying local to my roots, and working in equally small, nearby towns. After working many dead-end retail jobs, it finally dawned on me that I was not satisfied with the direction that my life was headed. My life had no direction nor excitement, just mental and intellectual roadblocks. It was then that I decided to take a leap of faith and return to school after a long hiatus period. I graduated from community college in 2020 with my associate in arts and transferred to Cal State for the spring semester. Since then, my passion for social justice and advocacy has continued to grow and I have found a purpose in life.

This statement has some good things going for it, but also some major problems. The student got caught up in telling their whole story instead of focusing on the larger point—that they are an awesome student who belongs in the program they are applying to. Like so many of us, the student was worried that some aspects of their record would be seen negatively, so they wanted to tell a story of a turnaround: I was having a hard time, got bad grades, but found my purpose and turned it all around. This isn't a bad story, but look at what the majority of the space in the paragraph is devoted to—it's almost exclusively about the struggles and very little about the turnaround, about who they are now and what they currently bring to the table. Compare that to where the student ended up after a process of several drafts:

> My passion for social justice stems from within. I am a first-generation college student and the eldest daughter of immigrant parents. While growing up I quickly became mindful of the challenges my family was facing. My parents made very little money while struggling to meet the needs of their three children. Being the eldest enabled me to see my parents' financial struggle and how it exhausted their mental health. Soon after, I became a caregiver for my siblings because my parents could not afford a sitter. I was forced to grow up sooner than I wanted and took on adult responsibilities. It is my ultimate goal to make my parents proud, overcome adversity, and meet my educational goals. Being a survivor of abuse has also inspired me to advocate for others. I am aware of the long-term negative effects abuse can have on people. Since coming to terms with my trauma and initiating a healing process, I am certain that social justice is my calling. My personal and familial struggles have caused me to fall down and come back stronger. Some days I wanted to give up, but I am proud that I persevered. My struggles are what incite my passion for social justice.

This version is a lot better. The student brings up many of the same issues but, rather than focusing on the struggle, pays more attention to where the student is now. This gives the reader a reason for reading the information about the student's background. The student tells the reader how the struggles inspired them, sparking their motivation and determination to succeed despite the odds. This version talks a lot more about what the student brings to the table and how their past will influence what they will do in the program. Additionally, notice in the first draft that the student is trying to preempt any criticism of their early school performance by talking about the issue that they had when they started community college. I understand the impulse. The student had bad grades in junior college and wanted the reader to know that those grades are not reflective of who they are now. This is fine, but the reader will always pay attention to what you point out. Doing what this student did in the early draft is just drawing a big red circle around their early grades and saying, "Please don't pay attention to those!" In the final draft, the student doesn't bother with explaining away early grades. Instead they focus on who they are now, what they can do, and why their past experiences will make them effective in the program they are applying to.

Let's look at another example, from the middle of a personal statement essay.

> My first semester in college at Cal State was a challenging experience. As a first-generation college student living far from home in a new city, I struggled to balance the responsibility of working and studying as a full-time student. I could tell how the stress from my studies was impacting my mental well-being and physical health. I connected with the Counseling and Psychological Resource Center and met with a counselor. The university paired me with a peer mentor who met with me weekly to discuss my grades, assignments, and strategies for improvement. This experience taught me valuable skills, including communicating professionally with my professors and utilizing campus resources effectively. Teaming with a mentor kept me accountable, and having someone to cheer me on opened my eyes to see that social workers can connect and understand the challenges faced by the populations they serve.
>
> In 2022, I became a mother and decided to move back to the Central Valley, transferring to California State University, Stanislaus. At Stanislaus, I found an uplifting academic community. Through my rigorous courses I encountered supportive and dedicated professors such as Dr. X, Dr. Y, and Dr. Z who challenged me to become a better student. Juggling the responsibilities of being a new mother while pursuing my bachelor's degree has been unpredictable. Thankfully, these professors understood that sometimes motherhood can interfere with your studies and were flexible. Last semester, I earned a spot on the dean's list with a 3.55 GPA in my sociology courses and an overall GPA of 3.2. My accomplishments could not have been possible without the relentless support of my family and classmates. It would make me proud to motivate other students to continue their studies because my story is a testament that hard work pays off in the end.
>
> These experiences have combined to shape my vision for a career in social work in a way nothing else could. Above all, I am committed to creating safe and supportive environments for students and their families, providing needed resources and support. My passion lies in working with children and young adults who face challenges similar to those I have overcome, ensuring that no child feels unheard or unsupported. I reflect these values with my daughter by allowing her to express her creativity through painting, drawing, and sculpting. As a social worker, I would love to support youth to enjoy the arts who may not have the same opportunities at home. In my free time, I volunteer at Delhi High School to help

raise funds for clubs and extracurricular activities. I am also a part of a grassroots organization called Central Valley Black, Indigenous, and People of Color Coalition. Our organization raises funds for mutual aid projects, and we hold different drives collecting warm clothes for the winter, food, and toys for the holiday seasons. Every family deserves access to the tools they need to thrive, and I strive to be part of that solution.

If allowed to pursue the master of social work degree from Stanislaus State, I know I could accomplish more since the institution's goals align with mine. The sociology courses I have taken have been instrumental in developing my academic and professional skills. I engaged with abstract theories in my Classical and Contemporary Sociological Theory classes and regularly prepared detailed synopses to deepen my understanding. In Research Methods, I learned how to conduct interviews and gather research data effectively, which enhanced my analytical and investigative abilities. My Social Inequalities class offered eye-opening insights into how systemic injustice can perpetuate inequality. As part of this course, we maintained a daily journal to reflect on the material and conduct deeper analyses, which enriched our classroom discussions and honed my critical thinking skills. A course on Child Abuse and Neglect provided practical knowledge for working with children, including how to identify signs of abuse and the proper procedures for reporting it. Studying sociology allowed me to understand how social systems work at the macro level and how they can impact us as individuals. These skills that I have acquired in my undergrad will help me adjust to the rigors of the master's program and excel in my studies.

There is a lot of good information in this section. The student talks about their experiences in their undergraduate program and the skills they learned that will help them in a graduate program. They also highlight personal experiences with volunteer work. But there are some real issues here, too. Notice how they go down the same path as the previous student, trying to explain away some lower grades from early in their college career. The rest of the essay is well written but poorly organized. The student jumps around, from talking about their education in paragraph two, then moving on to volunteer work in the next paragraph, then returning to education in paragraph three. The material they are writing about is fine, but the going back and forth between topics can leave the reader confused and less likely to retain the information the applicant wants them to focus on. The following rewrite is much better organized.

Academic Success at Stanislaus

In 2022, I became a mother and decided to move back to the Central Valley, transferring to California State University, Stanislaus. At Stanislaus, I found an uplifting academic community. Through my rigorous courses, I encountered supportive and dedicated professors such as Dr. X, Dr. Y, and Dr. Z, who challenged me to become a better student. Juggling the responsibilities of being a new mother while pursuing my bachelor's degree has been unpredictable. Thankfully, these professors understood that sometimes motherhood can interfere with your studies and were flexible. Last semester, I earned a spot on the dean's list with a 3.55 GPA in my sociology courses and an overall GPA of 3.2. My accomplishments could not have been possible without the relentless support of my family and classmates. It would make me proud to motivate other students to continue their studies because my story shows that hard work pays off.

Undergraduate Experiences in Sociology

The sociology courses I have taken have been instrumental in developing my academic and professional skills. I engaged with abstract theories in my Classical and Contemporary Sociological Theory classes and regularly prepared detailed synopses to deepen my understanding. In Research Methods, I learned how to conduct interviews and gather research data effectively, which enhanced my analytical and investigative abilities. My Social Inequalities class offered eye-opening insights into how systemic injustice can perpetuate inequality. As part of this course, we maintained a daily journal to reflect on the material and conduct deeper analyses, which enriched our classroom discussions and honed my critical thinking skills. A course on Child Abuse and Neglect provided practical knowledge for working with children, including how to identify signs of abuse and the proper procedures for reporting it. Studying sociology allowed me to understand how social systems work at the macro level and how they can impact us as individuals. These skills that I have acquired in my undergrad will help me adjust to the rigors of the master's program and excel in my studies.

Active Community Involvement

These experiences have combined to shape my vision for a career in social work in a way nothing else could. Above all, I am committed to creating safe and supportive environments for students and their families, providing needed resources and support. My passion lies in working

> with children and young adults who face challenges similar to those I have overcome, ensuring that no child feels unheard or unsupported. I reflect thesc values with my daughter by allowing her to express her creativity through painting, drawing, and sculpting. As a social worker, I would love to support youth to enjoy the arts who may not have the same opportunities at home. In my free time, I volunteer at Delhi High School to help raise funds for clubs and extracurricular activities. I am also a part of a grassroots organization called Central Valley Black, Indigenous, and People of Color Coalition. Our organization raises funds for mutual aid projects, and we hold different drives collecting warm clothes for the winter, food, and toys for the holiday seasons. Every family deserves access to the tools they need to thrive, and I strive to be part of that solution. If allowed to pursue the master's of social work degree from Stanislaus State, I know I could accomplish more since the institution's goals align with mine.

There is a lot to like in this new version of the essay. At the end of each paragraph, the student reminds the reader why this section aligns with the bigger thesis of the essay, and the organization puts similar material together in an order that makes sense. The student also starts this section focusing on their academic success rather than trying to explain away a rougher period. There is a time and a place to talk about past academic struggles, and this is probably not that time or place. If you do bring up those issues, it should always be in service of showcasing a positive trait that your previous struggles highlight, like perseverance, work ethic, or ability to overcome adversity.

Lastly, I want to look at an example of how we can stay true to a core story but focus on aspects that highlight why we belong in a particular program. This is a first-draft introduction from a student applying to an educational counseling program:

> Growing up as a first-generation Latina college student, my family and I have faced many trials and tribulations to get to this point. My family migrated to the United States with aspirations of a better life for themselves and future generations. I remember growing up listening to my mother stress the importance of obtaining an education to have opportunities she never had the chance to pursue. At a young age, my mother had no choice but to grow up quickly and selflessly put aside the plans and goals she had for herself to provide all she could for my siblings and me. Growing up as the oldest sibling of four, I have taken the sacrifices and

> challenges my mother has made very personally and have committed to make her proud and serve as a mentor to my younger siblings.

There is nothing wrong with this statement, but nothing in it relates specifically to counseling or the connection that the student has with it. Obviously, the student's connection to family is important to them, and it comes across that the student takes education seriously, but any hint of how this connects with being a counselor is vague at best. Here's the final draft, which was the sixth revision:

> Navigating the college experience can be tricky when being the first in your family to attend. Despite having no guidance when first applying, I had the privilege of having a high school guidance counselor named Adriana, who eventually became a mentor and was very willing to guide me throughout my journey from high school to college. My mentor's unconditional support has inspired me to go into a counseling career because I felt that my transition was very smooth due to having her by my side. She helped me become the best mentor I could for anyone in my family that had questions about college. Suddenly I found myself guiding my younger siblings, cousins, and friends as they filled out college and FAFSA applications, and making sure they were registering for the correct classes. Walking through uncharted territories was very hard on me but I am glad I was able to make that process a lot easier for my siblings and cousins. I am excited to continue serving as a mentor through your counseling program and become a counselor as part of my career. My professional background as a nursing assistant and my academic background, obtaining a bachelor's degree in sociology, will make me an excellent candidate for your program.

This version changes the focus from the student's mother to the student's relationship with a high school guidance counselor. When I read the first draft, I really liked the idea of the student talking about the struggles and sacrifices that their family member made to enable them to finish college. The problem is that the focus was not on the student and their goals for the new program. This new version brings up the story of the student's mother later in the essay, but puts focus on the student, their motivation for going into counseling, and the skills they bring to the table that will make them a strong candidate for the program.

9

THE CV

MOST APPLICATIONS WILL ASK FOR a copy of your CV. If you're like me, you'll say to yourself, "No problem, I know exactly what a CV is"—and then frantically look it up on the internet. CV, it turns out, stands for curriculum vitae, and that's Latin . . . at least I think it's Latin. Anyway, all it really means in this context is an academic résumé. You've probably put together a work résumé for yourself at some point, and a CV is not much different. Instead of work experience, this one will focus on academic experience and on other experiences relevant to the program you are applying to.

From the perspective of what you're trying to do with your application, the CV is just another extension of your story. Your application package, when it's done, should be a set of materials that together tell a coherent story about you and your potential for doing well in the program. Your CV should be a natural extension of the story that you've started to tell in the other sections. If you've been emphasizing aspects of your background and experience in your statement and in your letters of recommendation, then you should make sure you are touching on these again in your CV.

In other words, the CV is basically a quick guide to information that you discuss in more depth in other parts of your application. Your CV is also a great place to highlight areas of your experience or your education that you want to make sure get the reader's attention.

Quick example. I was working with a student recently who had an overall GPA around 2.5. However, as with a lot of first-gen students, his GPA for recent semesters, once he started taking his major classes and some upper-division classes, was a lot higher. He wasn't sure how to talk about that shift in his application package. When the readers got his information, the overall GPA would be there for them to see, but the fact that he'd been earning excellent grades over the past two years wasn't really reflected in that number.

The CV is a great way to retell the story of this student's GPA in a way that matches how he's been performing recently. When we talked about putting his CV together, one suggestion was to emphasize, near the very beginning, his "upper-division GPA" or his "major GPA." You may need to use one of the online GPA calculators and your transcript to find out what this is, but once you calculate it, make sure to put it front and center. We aren't hiding your overall GPA from the readers; they can see it on your transcripts and elsewhere on the application. But the CV is a place for you to provide an interpretation of that GPA. There is no rule that you must write, "Overall GPA 2.5, but major GPA 3.7." If you have a better GPA in upper-division classes or in your major, just write "major GPA 3.7" and leave it at that. While being clear what the number represents, so that the reader won't confuse this with your overall GPA, give them a quick and easy way to contextualize or recontextualize that overall GPA number, depending on whether they've seen it yet.

EDUCATIONAL EXPERIENCE

When students get to the part of the CV where they need to talk about their education, they often get hung up. For some reason, many draw a blank when asked to talk about the skills they learned as an undergraduate. As a former community college student, I think I get what's happening here. For a lot of first-generation students, college can be extremely overwhelming when we first start. There is so much to figure out, so many things to try and learn, not to mention passing classes. Once you start to understand how things work and get the hang of managing your schedule, studying for classes, writing essays, and more, passing classes feels a lot easier. By the time you're ready to graduate, you're not struggling nearly as much as you did earlier in your college career, and because of that, you get the impression that what you're doing is easy, or at least easier than what you were doing when you first started. You don't really notice all the growth you've had to go through to get to the point where passing classes seems easy. You don't notice all the new skills you've developed. Right now, my son is twelve. He's growing all the time, and recently his voice has started to change. My wife and I have watched as his body and his personality have changed over time, all the time. But from his perspective, he doesn't even notice. This happens to everyone. Because we experience life as ourselves every day, we don't see the scope of the changes we've gone through or the skills we've developed when these changes occur over the course of years.

That can put us in a tough spot when we go to write the CV. What skills are you supposed to write about when you don't even recognize the skills you've developed? Let's think about it a little bit, though. Even generally speaking, you've had to learn a lot of things and master a lot of skills to make it this far.

PROJECT MANAGEMENT You've had to manage multiple competing time schedules and levels of urgency across various classes and various timelines. You've had to learn to prioritize your tasks, plan out your time, and find ways to meet the multiple expectations of different people all at once. That's a skill, or set of skills.

RESEARCH This one should be a given. You've likely had to do quite a bit of research to pass many of your classes, so it's a skill you should certainly discuss here. You may feel that something like this might be "taken for granted" or that anyone with a bachelor's degree would have this skill. That's true in a way, but as I've mentioned before in the personal statement section, if it's not in your materials then it doesn't exist. While it may be true that most students who are graduating with a bachelor's degree have some research skills, you should still make it a point to tell your reader that this is part of what *you* bring to the table. Imagine getting two résumés. On one, the person lists "bachelor's degree" and assumes that we understand the skills and background that are needed to achieve this. The second résumé doesn't assume that we know and instead spells out the skills they learned as part of their degree, skills like research. It may be true that both candidates have the same skill set, but the person who takes the time to describe what they've studied and what they can do will have an advantage.

WRITING Much as with the research element, people often overlook how much practice they have had to put into their writing over the course of earning a bachelor's degree. You have had to practice multiple different types of writing, for different audiences and for different goals. Make sure to talk a little bit about the skills you gained in this area.

ANALYSIS The specifics can really change from one major to the next, but everyone, from English majors to biology majors, has had to practice different types of analysis, whether theoretical analysis, data analysis, or both. Talk about some of the courses you took in which you practiced these skills, and any projects, papers, or assignments that developed them for you.

PRACTICAL TIPS

Make a list of all the upper-division classes you took. If you can, get a copy of the syllabus for each class, then list out all the things you had to do to pass each class. Was there a special research project you had to do, were there papers you had to write, journals you had to work on? List out as much as you can for each of the classes. Once you're done, go through and see which of the things you listed are good matches for the skill sets that you think make you a good fit for the program you are applying to. Are you applying to a program that requires a lot of memorization? Maybe you took a class with lots of terms and equations that you had to memorize to pass. Will the program you are applying to require a lot of analysis or research skills? Then look for projects or papers that required you to apply theory, create a research proposal, or develop analytical skills. The goal here is to get your brain working on all the skills you developed over the course of your undergraduate career and get those skills down on paper. Once they are there, you can start to decide which of those skill sets you want to highlight.

Remember!

When you write out a skill set on your CV, you are not advertising to a program that you are necessarily an expert on that topic. Sometimes, students worry about listing things on their CV because they feel that even though they passed a class called "statistics," they may not really remember a lot from that class, and if they put it on the CV, someone may decide later to sit them in front a computer and say, "Do some statistics for me right now! You said you could do it on your CV, so let's see!" That's not ever going to happen, and being an expert is also not what you are advertising when you put a skill on your CV. The people reading your application know that you're not an expert in these areas. Taking an undergraduate course is rarely enough to make anyone an expert in anything. Instead, what you are telling the reader is that when you were asked to learn some difficult concepts involving statistics, you were able to do it. You took a class that required you to think in a particular way, abstractly, analytically, mathematically, and you were able to do it. By putting that on your CV, you are saying, "I did it once, I can do it again." And you can! Remember the main things the readers want to know: Can this person do well in our classes? Can this person do well in this career? By listing the skills you needed to practice in order to pass courses as an undergraduate, you are letting them know that you have been called on in the past to learn this particular way of thinking and you were able to do it—and so, most likely, if their program asks you to do it again, you'll be able to.

Finding CV Examples Online

The first thing most of us do when we don't know something is look it up online. That's totally fine in this case, too. However, let me give you a heads up about looking for CV examples online. The people who are most motivated to put up their CVs online are the people who have impressive things that they want to show off. Right now, if you search for undergraduate CV examples on Google, you'll find a ton of material, but most of it is going to be from people who went to a fancy school like Yale or who have the kind of credits that come with going to a fancy school, like publications with a researcher, research assistantships, or various awards and scholarships. All those things are great, but if you are looking for examples of what a normal CV might look like for someone who hasn't gone to an Ivy League school, unfortunately there is going to be less available. Often, the examples online will be intimidating and discouraging. They will make you feel like you don't have anything to put on your CV if you don't have awards and accolades like the people in the examples you are finding, but that's not the case.

The reality is that going to an expensive school like Harvard or Yale can get you a lot of things that going to a state school may not—like impressive-sounding awards, the opportunity to be a lab assistant for a big-time researcher and get your name on a publication in the process, or being attached to well-funded projects with academic superstars. That's all great, but it can leave the rest of us, who didn't go to that sort of school, feeling self-conscious about the things we have listed on our own CV, which may seem less impressive.

What you should know is that regular people from state schools get into graduate programs all the time. Grad programs are not only filled with people who have amazing awards and impressive titles. They are also filled with thousands of everyday people who have the same types of accomplishments that you have. The key to writing a good CV is not having a million amazing titles or awards. It's about really considering what the people reading your application want to know about you and finding ways to present the experience that you have in ways that match those expectations.

Let me give you an example that I use in my workshops all the time. One of my students was applying to pursue a master's degree in counseling at our local state university. Even though Cal State Stanislaus isn't Princeton, a lot of people apply to the graduate programs here each year, and the master's program in counseling routinely gets two or three times more applications than they have available seats for incoming students. With those odds, you would imagine that students are constantly worried that someone else out there has a more impressive CV with better internships at more prestigious places, or some amazing awards to impress the readers. The student I was working with didn't have those things to put on her CV, so we had to think carefully about what the program she was applying to wanted to know about her. We talked about her academic career and the things that she had done in classes, and we found ways to match those experiences to qualities that the program might be seeking in a candidate. The most interesting thing was in her section on outside experience. She didn't have any internships that came with a formal title through a well-known organization, so instead she listed two things that I think were smart and a great fit for the program she was applying to: babysitting and helping a family member through a crisis.

At first glance, neither of those things would be a first choice to go on a CV. Babysitting isn't impressive in itself—lots of people do it all the time, and it's not directly related to academic work. Helping a family member through a crisis is even less formal—no one paid her for that, there was no boss, no one with an important title who could write her a letter of recommendation, and there is no office to call for a reference. However, those two entries on her CV, along with her explanation of *why* they mattered, were smart inclusions. Look at how she described her work as a babysitter:

- Enforced rules and managed behavior through developmentally appropriate discipline.
- Applied positive behavior management techniques to enhance social interactions and emotional development.
- Discussed children's behavior with parents and developed a plan on how to handle situations when needed.

All the ways she described her work as a babysitter matched well with the things she would be learning to do as a counselor. One thing you might notice is the professional-sounding language that she used to describe, basically, "keeping the kids from destroying the house" and "doing my best to calm them down when they got rowdy" and "talking to the parents about the best way to deal with their kids." Where did she get the language she used to describe the work she had done? Great question! *She read the website of the program she was applying to.* She clicked through on some of the example job listings they had posted, she saw the language that hiring organizations were using in their job descriptions, and she took that vocabulary and applied it to her own experiences. Here's a line from one of those job listings for a high school counselor: "Establishes with teachers and school administration standards of pupil behavior through proper control and supervision." Sounds a lot like some of what she wrote, doesn't it? Now look at how she described helping a family member through a crisis:

> *2018–Current. Independent, Central Valley CA*
> **Caregiver**
>
> - Helped family member through trauma of sexual abuse
> - Monitored her to ensure no attempts of self-harm
> - Provided her information on experiences after sexual abuse
> - Provided her emotional support especially through anxiety attacks of PTSD

Same strategy. She took an actual experience from her life and described it using the language of the profession she was applying to study. This was an amazingly smart idea. She didn't have multiple internships with big nonprofits in the Central Valley, so she showed the qualities that she needed to show in the most inventive way possible.

To be sure, there can be downsides to using an unconventional style on your CV. There is always the chance that a reader will be critical of these types of entries, considering them unprofessional. However, that's a risk no matter what type of entries you have on your CV. Our plan here is to submit the best possible view of the work that you have done and give the best interpretation of why that work will make you a good candidate in the program. How they will interpret the information that you give them is out of your hands. If you do have impressive-looking internships, you can go through a similar process, explaining the work you did in similar language. If you haven't had the chance to have one of those internships yet, then I think that using this method can help you explain the experience you bring to the table.

Using Your Work Experience

I know that it's tempting to put your work experience from outside of the university on a CV, especially if you feel that other areas are light on material. However, generally I would say that your time, and the space of the application, is better spent on describing your academic experience than on listing your various part-time jobs. I'm not saying that you didn't work hard at those jobs. I've worked long hours on the McDonald's drive-thru and the Taco Bell burrito assembly line myself. But the CV should really be focused on experiences that are directly related to the type of work you will be doing as a grad student and as a professional after you graduate. If you have work experience that is relevant to either of those, you should list it. If not, then consider whether there might be other things to talk about that better give an idea of what you bring to the table.

Connect to Your Other Materials and Stay Consistent

No matter what experiences you list on your CV, be ready to link those experiences to your other application materials. If you have a solid internship on your CV, make sure that you are talking about it in your statement of purpose, and vice versa. Make sure to point out the areas that you believe are your strong ones to your letter writers as well, and mention that you would appreciate them touching on those subjects in their letters.

This is especially true if you are using nontraditional examples of your experience, as in the CV example above with the babysitting and caregiver experiences. Those are going to work best if they are also described in detail in the personal statement. You can add detail there that isn't in the CV and go into an explanation of why these experiences are a good fit for the program you are applying to. The idea is that you want a coherent narrative that spans across all your application documents. Each of the pieces of the application should support the others. If you are describing your GPA in one way in your statement, be sure to describe it in the same way in the CV.

NEXT STEPS

Now that we've talked through how to put together a CV, we'll turn to a piece of the application that not everyone will need but that many programs ask for: a writing sample. We'll talk about what programs are looking for, what type of sample you should submit. and ways to make your writing stand out.

10

WRITING SAMPLES AND TESTING

MANY PROGRAMS WILL ASK FOR a writing sample as part of your application package, especially if you are applying to a PhD program. As we've discussed in regard to other parts of the book, you should consider carefully, when choosing a writing sample, what the program is looking for in a candidate. Every program wants to know that a candidate will be able to do the academic work needed to pass their classes. It's a solid bet that most graduate programs will involve a fair amount of writing, though the types of writing that different programs require can vary drastically. In sociology, our research requires both a technical type of writing, when discussing data, methods, and analysis, and a more approachable and narrative form when we are describing the social circumstances and situations. From that perspective, sociology programs that require a writing sample are probably looking to see if you can handle those two kinds of writing to some degree, so the sample you give them should have aspects of both. A nursing program or a math program or a computer science program may want only a more technical type of writing, while narrative writing may not be high on their list of candidate abilities.

First, talk to your team members. Tell them exactly what the application is asking for in terms of your writing sample. Your team should be able to give you good insights into the type of writing the program you're applying to will want to see and whether the pieces you have are a good match. Another great source of information is the department you are applying to. Talk to someone in the department about the writing sample to find out more about what their readers are looking for.

One big thing that any program is going to be looking for is how well you communicate through writing. This has to do with content, but it has more to do with how clearly you can write and communicate ideas to a reader. What this means, practically speaking, is that you should do your best to go over your writing sample with a fine-toothed comb to pick out any grammar or spelling mistakes before it goes out. The writing sample is something that will be overlooked by a lot of students who have run out of time toward the end of the semester and don't have the energy to go through their application looking for issues. If you can make time for it, your writing sample will stand out in a good way, no matter what it's about, by virtue of being mistake free. Another good idea is to ask your college writing center to help you edit for grammar, spelling, and clarity. Having multiple sets of eyes on all parts of your application is always good, but here it is crucial. Just proofreading the writing sample yourself is fine in a pinch, but, because you wrote it and you know the ideas you are trying to communicate, your brain is going to automatically fill in a lot of gaps in your writing on its own as you read. Have you ever seen that meme that writes something in a weird way, but your brain can still tell what it says? "Aoccdrnig to rscheearch at Cmabrigde uinervtisy, it deosn't mttaer waht oredr the ltteers in a wrod are, the olny iprmoetnt tihng is taht the frist and lsat ltteres are at the rghit pclae. The rset can be a tatol mses and you can sitll raed it wouthit a porbelm. Tihs is bcuseae we do not raed ervey lteter by itslef but the wrod as a wlohe."

What that (sort of) says is not completely true, apparently. There was no study at Cambridge University, and there is more to it than just keeping the first and last letters in the right place, but the larger point is that if our brain is expecting something to go a certain way, it will fill in the gaps even if a word is spelled wrong, or in the wrong order. If you're reading your own writing, you are going to be a lot more susceptible to this than another person because you know what's coming next, and you know what you are trying to communicate. Even though *your* brain will skip over some of these mistakes, they will likely stand out as red flags to other people who read it, especially people on the admission committee. Having another person look over all of the writing in your application will help catch these issues, and if others haven't had time to take this step, it will give your application an advantage. Another way to catch these types of mistakes is to read your work out loud. This is good advice for *all* material, not just the writing sample. Reading aloud is another way to short-circuit your brain's ability to skip over missing or misspelled words and grammar mistakes. When you read aloud, you are forcing yourself to read more carefully, and sections that have a missing word, an awkward phrase, or bad grammar will stand out in a way that they might not if you were reading silently to yourself.

WHERE TO GET A WRITING SAMPLE

The obvious source is papers that you've written for past classes. However, you are under no obligation to keep those papers exactly as previously written when you use them in your application. When I was working on my first set of applications, I remember thinking that it might be cheating if I went through the writing sample and fixed any errors that were in the original paper or added a paragraph or idea. That's not the case at all. You are not required to turn in a writing sample exactly as it was when you turned it in for a class. Rather, the point is to provide the best possible representation of your writing skills. That includes editing for clarity, spelling, punctuation, and grammar.

The best choice for a writing sample is something you've already written that is not so specialized to a particular class or topic that it will require much explanation. The readers may not be familiar with a topic or theory mentioned in your sample, even if they are in that discipline. Theoretically, it shouldn't matter too much if they don't have background on what you're writing, but it may be a bad choice if the topic is super-specific or refers to something that was talked about in class but that may not be widely known. If you still have it, include the prompt that was given for the assignment, which will help orient your readers to what you are writing about and why.

Go through the sample and do a triple check for spelling and grammar issues and another check for clarity. It would be a good idea to have someone who wasn't in the class or who doesn't have a background in the subject read the sample. This will help give you a sense of whether it will be clear to the readers without the original context. Your readers on the admission committee will be experts in their field, but that doesn't mean that they are experts in *every* field that a writing sample might cover, so have a reader confirm that your sample provides enough context or background information for ready comprehension.

It may also be good to expand the original paper with new ideas. Chances are that any writing you have is from a past class, and since then you've either taken new classes or at least finished the class you wrote the paper for. You can use your later insights to expand the paper in a new direction and give a perspective that you may not have had when you originally wrote it.

CONFERENCE PRESENTATION STRATEGY

This last tip may come a little late for people who are working on their applications in the fall, but for those of you who are planning ahead or who may need to do this process again, think about submitting a paper you are writing or revising to use as your writing sample to an undergraduate section in an academic conference. I know that probably sounds horrifying to a lot of you—the idea of submitting your work for *more* judgment and critique. But the undergraduate sections of academic conferences can be a lot less intimidating than you might think. At most conferences, people present works in progress at what are called roundtables, where a small group of people who have written on a similar subject each take turns presenting their paper or their research.

There usually isn't an audience, or if there is one it's friends and family of someone presenting. The nice thing is that when you participate in an undergraduate roundtable session, the others at your table are most likely as nervous and scared as you are. You will be asked to talk about your paper for ten to fifteen minutes max, and the reality is that while you are talking, everyone else at the table is either dreading that their turn to present is coming up or completely zoned out from the adrenaline dump of having just presented. People will pay attention to what you say, but no one is going to be so invested that they try to pick apart your paper or ask you impossibly hard questions about theory or data. I can't say that would *never* happen, and someone, somewhere might try that, but I can say that in the fifteen years I've been presenting at conferences I've never seen it happen. Most people are supportive, nervous, and just happy to get through their own presentations. After you present, you'll not only have a writing sample to submit, but you'll be able to say on your CV that you've presented your work at an academic conference.

Not all conferences are huge affairs that take place at a fancy convention center or hotel. For every big national conference, there are many regional conferences that happen at a university campus or a Holiday Inn somewhere. The important thing is not how fancy the conference sounds (though, if you are feeling bold, apply to the undergrad section of a big national conference—it will look extra impressive). The point is that you put yourself out there and started engaging in the academic process, something that very few of the other applicants are going to be able to say.

At many universities, your academic department or college will offer funding to students to attend these conferences, either to pay up front for some travel expenses or reimburse you for them. At my university, the dean's office often has money for student presentations at conferences, and every year they have a hard time finding students to give it to. Most students are just like you and really intimidated by the process, so they just avoid it. If you can muster up the courage, in many cases you'll find that there are support services you will be able to draw on that are going unused because students either don't know they are there or assume that any financial supports will be ultra-competitive and they don't want to put themselves in a position to be rejected. I get it, no one wants to be rejected, but the reality is that in many circumstances you may be competing with far fewer people than you think, some of whom are probably unprepared. In a surprising number of cases, you may not be competing with anyone at all, in which case you get the award or the support or the grant by default! Being bold can pay off in a lot of ways that you may never have imagined.

TESTING

I am not going to go into too much depth about the various tests that may be required by the programs you are applying to. There are other books that go into these tests in more detail and with better advice than I would be able to cover here. Instead, I want to mention a few things that others may not know and some ways to think about the tests as a whole. The first is that you need to really consider your application in the big picture when deciding how much time to devote to studying for a test, if one is required. Some programs, like law schools or medical schools, put enormous emphasis on test scores, so it makes sense that devoting a lot of your time to studying and preparing for the tests should be a priority. Many PhD programs put emphasis on GRE scores, but how much emphasis may vary from program to program. Getting information about how big a role the test scores play in the admission evaluation is a big part of determining how much time to spend. If testing is not as big a part of the application process, then you may want to devote more of your time to working on your personal and research statements.

Planning how much time you need to devote to test prep is also a question of your personal relationship with testing. For some reason, there are those of us who have an easy time taking multiple-choice tests and those of us who really struggle. In my experience, these struggles can be especially pronounced for people who did not grow up with English as their primary language. So many of these tests can rely on understanding small nuances in word choice and differences in phrasing. For people who grew up speaking only English, these will be much easier to spot. If multiple-choice tests just don't agree with you at all and you know that doing well will be a struggle, consider whether it would be worth delaying your application in order to prep and study for the test. This may be especially true for programs that require highly specialized tests with skills that may have not been covered in your undergraduate program. My wife took the LSAT before she applied to law school. That test is insane. There are odd word problems, logic tests, and overall baffling questions that require time and energy to figure out. Don't make the mistake of thinking that you can just "common sense" your way through these exams.

Many of them have their own strange logic that you need to study for specifically.

If you are applying to a master's program, if they require testing, in most cases it will be the GRE. If you are short on time, using a GRE study guide may be the best way to go. There are several online study options that are helpful, but many people don't know that university libraries often carry test prep books that will otherwise cost a lot of money if you buy them new. Similarly, once people take a test and apply, they will often sell their used materials for a lot less money than when buying on Amazon new, so keep your eyes open. Make flash cards of the most used vocabulary words. Many of them you will recognize and not need to study, but there are going to be a lot of words that none of use in normal, everyday speech, and learning those definitions will really help. Also make flash cards of the most used formulas for the math section. Many of us will remember the formula for a right triangle, but what about for a sphere or a cylinder? Those equations are not complex, but if you don't remember what they are it will be difficult to do those problems.

My philosophy on testing is that you should find out what the average score is for people who are admitted into the programs you are applying to and have that be your target. If you hit that target, then the time and work you put into the other materials, such as your personal statement, will have a chance to shine. Like the GPA, a test score is just a number, and at the end of the day the admission committee members are going to read *a lot* of different names and numbers, so keeping test scores and GPA straight in their heads will be hard. But a unique story and strong letters will stand out when numbers blur together. Other people may have a different take on this and make different calculations about what is more important. It's a really good idea to talk to as many people as you can to get perspective on the particular types of programs you are applying to and hear the strategies that may have worked for others in similar positions.

NEXT STEPS

In the next section, we'll go into letters of recommendation. This is often one of the most dreaded parts of the application process, alongside the statement of purpose. Talking to professors about letters can be awkward, and that potential for embarrassment can lead to procrastination. We'll talk about the letters, what should go in them, talking to professors, and your role in the whole process.

11

LETTERS OF RECOMMENDATION

WE TALKED A BIT ABOUT letters of recommendation in chapter 4, on building a mentorship team. Hopefully, by this point in the process, you've been talking to team members about your graduate school plans and have in mind a few professors and possibly others who can provide letters. In this chapter, we'll go through everything you need to know about letters of recommendation and how to bring up the subject with the people on your team.

PLANNING FOR YOUR LETTERS

How Many Letters Do You Need, and Who Should Write Them?

Most programs will ask for three letters of recommendation, though occasionally I've seen programs ask for only two, or allow you to submit a fourth letter if you have one. No matter the program you're applying to, the admission committee will want to know that you can do the academic work required by the program and that you are capable of going on to be a good professional in the field. The people best positioned to talk about your academic qualifications will be your professors. Typically, at least two of your letters of recommendation should be from professors you've been communicating with and who have agreed to be part of your mentorship team. In considering your options for a third letter, consider what the program will be training you for. If you're going into a PhD program that will prepare you to be a professor, all three of your letters should be from professors. However, if the program will train you for a professional field outside of the university, like counseling, teaching, or social work, it may be a good idea to have a letter from someone who can talk from professional or personal experience about your ability to work in the field.

For many of us, that person might be a supervisor of an internship or a boss at a job—someone who can tell the admission committee that you possess qualities that will make you a good professional once you graduate. What it means to be a good professional in a field will vary from one program to another. Look back at the process in chapter 8 for developing your personal statement, where you thought up a few adjectives that describe a good professional working in your desired field. Who in your life can speak about your ability to meet those criteria? You need just one letter writer in this category—your other two letters should be from professors. Your application is going to a graduate program run by professors, after all, some of whom will be reading your materials, and so your letters need to come primarily from people who speak their language.

What Are Schools Looking For, and What Goes into the Letters?

In the big picture, we should think about letters of recommendation as another component of an integrated application package. In a good application, each part of the package will support the other pieces. We want to make sure that major positive aspects of our record are highlighted in all the materials, including the letters, and that each of the pieces of the application helps to build the story about us that we want to tell. Often, students think about the letters as a sort of black box. You ask for the letter, and then you have no control or even idea of what is going into them, what they say about you, or when they get submitted. This can *sometimes* be the case, but ideas about letters of recommendation vary somewhat from professor to professor, including how much input they may want from you and whether they will let you read the finished product before it's sent. Some professors prefer to keep their letters private. That is common, but I've also worked with many professors who let students read their letters and give feedback. Since communication is a big part of the process, it's totally fine to ask the professor their philosophy on this. If you feel comfortable in the communication between you and the professor, trust that they wouldn't take on this project if they weren't confident in your ability to perform well in graduate school. *However*, if you feel that you don't have a good idea whether one of your professors is going to write you a good letter, if the communication between you is shaky, or if you just get a strange feeling about it, you may want to consider looking for another person to ask.

What to Give the Team

Let me give you some inside information, from the other side of the desk. When we sit down to write a letter of recommendation, we professors are not suddenly flooded with memories of everything you've ever said in class or every paper you've ever written. In all actuality, we probably don't remember a whole lot of details apart from your general vibe and the overall impression you've made. That's not a comment on you—we have hundreds of students each year, and even the brightest ones can blend in with the crowd, given enough time. We need as much help as possible to give you what you need in your letter, so it's up to you to give us that help.

This will seem strange to some students who think of the letter as something that they have no influence over, but that isn't necessarily the case. You can absolutely talk to us about the letter, and you should definitely give us the materials we need in order to write an effective recommendation. We will often rely on those materials to fill in details about who you are and to support our arguments about your qualifications and preparation to take on the graduate program. If I agree to write you a letter of recommendation, I am basically saying that on the basis of my experience, I believe that you will be a good student in the program and that you have the potential to go on to be a good professional in your field. When I write about that in the letter, I need evidence for my perspective, so whatever you can give me to help make that case will add persuasive detail to the letter. In other words, you do have some amount of control over what gets talked about in your letter, and the more information you give me, the more I will have to put in. This can include big ideas that you want to touch on that are reflected in your other application materials, like a focus on your research skills or your history of volunteer work. Ask your team what aspects they think would be the most effective to highlight and what is needed to make a good case for each.

This is another good reason to bring your team members into the early stages of writing up your personal statement. Often, we want to give others only our most polished writing, but in your drafting process, you may have tried out and then deleted one or more personal stories that you decided didn't fit into the statement. That's fine, but those stories you've already edited out might be helpful to us in our letter writing, providing more relevant detail and useful insights into who you are as a person. As a rule, the more material we have to work with, the better.

LETTER WRITING PACKAGE

You should plan to give each of your letter writers a package of material. It should include your CV, your personal statement or statement of purpose, and a copy of your writing sample (if you need one). Lastly, and maybe most importantly, you need to give them an "About Me" page that lists any and everything that doesn't show up in those other documents. You can include interesting things you've done, hobbies you enjoy, places you've been, potentially relevant experiences. Think of it as your chance to give them enough raw materials to help personalize the letter of recommendation. When I was gathering letters from my own team members, some of them literally copied and pasted pieces of my "About Me" page into their letters. This may sound like cheating, but in reality, you're helping to make our job a little easier. We want to present you in the best possible light, and that's more likely when we have information that helps us paint a picture of you as a whole and complete person.

In addition, it can be helpful to give your letter writers the following information in a short document to refer to as needed while drafting the letter:

1. How long you've known them. Whether you only took a class from this professor in your freshman year or they have been your advisor for three semesters, remind them of the timeline and other context, which they may not recall off the top of their head.
2. How you performed in their class.
3. A list of each institution and program you are applying to.
4. How and when the letter needs to be submitted.
5. Anything specific they should know about a particular program that may be different from the others you are applying to.

SPECIAL NOTES FOR LETTER WRITERS WHO AREN'T PROFESSORS

If you have non-professor letter writers on your team, consider that they may never have written the type of letter of recommendation you need for your application. In the business world, letters of recommendation are often much shorter, sometimes amounting to "This person worked here from this date to this date and didn't steal anything." That's not always the case, but such letters typically don't contain the level of detail or the *types* of detail needed for a graduate program application. You should absolutely have a conversation with any outside letter writers you have and ask if they've written graduate application letters before. If they haven't, consider asking another member of your team if you can share their letter with this non-professor member as an example of what you need. If the other members are keeping their letters confidential, instead do your best to give this letter writer some guidance on what the application committee will want to know about you and your capabilities. This is good input to give any "outside" member of your team, especially if they are not familiar with the program you're applying to or the specific career path you're pursuing. The more detailed the letter, and the more it is tailored to the programs you're applying to, the better. Since outside team members may not have experience with what is expected, you need to help them!

SUBMITTING LETTERS

How Are Letters Submitted?

Nowadays, almost all letters of recommendation are submitted online through university portals. When you are filling out your application online, you will most likely come to a screen that asks you to submit the email addresses of your three letter writers. The applications department will send each an email letting them know that you have requested a letter and giving them instructions on how to submit it. Many departments will ask the letter writers a series of questions, asking them to rate you from 1 to 5 on how great you are at doing one thing or another. Once each writer has uploaded their letter, you will likely be sent an email confirming the submission, though in some instances you may need to log into the application portal to check. Once you see that a letter has been sent, be sure to send a follow-up thank you!

Timing

When you ask for the letters is an important thing to take into consideration. You should talk to your professors as soon as possible. Even if you are still a semester or more away from the application, you should bring professors on board now. The time you spend talking with them, planning for the future, and checking in will pay off. If you are in the fall semester of your application year, try to talk to each of your letter writers by September or October at the latest.

Each year, I have a few well-prepared students who come to my office hours sometime in October. They let me know where they are applying, they go through drafts of their personal statements, and they give me a heads up when applications are coming due. These students make life easy. There is also another group of students who talk to me about graduate school for the first time in early December, right before we leave for the holiday break. They often mention it once, then don't contact me again until a week before the due date or even later, when they finally have a statement written and can get me a copy. These students make life a little harder. Each year, I have students who wait until the last possible minute to ask for a letter, and while I do my best to accommodate everyone I can, the later I get the request, the harder it is to write a good letter.

You should strive to be that first sort of student, the one who makes life easy on their professors and plans ahead. If you think about it from our perspective, when crunch time hits, and we have ten letters to write in two days, whose letter do you think we will feel obligated to give the most time and attention to? If you were in our office early, gave us plenty of time for a heads up, and made sure to check in, you will be at the top of our list.

There are other reasons to check in early. If you send me your materials in October or November, there is plenty of time for me to help you catch mistakes or rewrite sections that don't sound quite right. If you wait until the last minute, you had better hope that you wrote a perfect first draft, because we're out of time.

Lastly, be aware that if your application is due in the winter months, especially in January, your professors will be hard to get in touch with over the holiday break. The crush of last-minute finals grading, getting grades in, and then having our normal schedules and routines overturned by the break—and perhaps having our kids home from school—will make our attention spans a lot shorter. Even if your professor is well intentioned, they are going to be less vigilant about returning emails quickly when there are holiday parties, last-minute shopping, and decorating to do. Get in early—don't count on all of your most important communication happening over the holiday break. That would only make things much harder.

Meeting Due Dates and Sending Reminders

You must be comfortable sending updates and reminders to your team. You know your due dates better than anyone else, while your professors are likely juggling multiple due dates across different programs and universities. I know that it can be intimidating, writing to a professor to let them know there is something they need to do, but to be honest, it can often be received more as a big help than as an annoyance. Many semesters, I have ten, twenty, or even more letters I to write for people in all kinds of programs with all kinds of due dates. Unfortunately, many students will request a letter from me once and then fall off the map when I say yes. I get it, they don't want to bother me, and they are worried that if they seem pushy or rude I will decide to not write them a letter after all. You'll have to fight this fear though, because you need these letters, and they have a definite due date. You can't just rely on the good will and excellent memory of every professor. You need to be proactive.

Even though you've given your professors everything they need to write the letters, you still need to take the reins on reminding them about upcoming dates. Set a reminder schedule for yourself. If you give your team members a letter package six weeks before the due date, send them a reminder in about two weeks, and later, when it's getting closer, send them a reminder every week until the deadline. I know this sounds a little pushy, but you have to account for the fact that professors are human and will forget things just as easily as anyone else, especially at the end of the fall semester and over the winter break, when most letters are due. Reminders don't need to be harsh—just a note with a gentle heads up that the deadline is coming up, and an offer to get them anything they may need to make writing your letter easier.

Not all your letters will necessarily have the same due date, so be sure to include a list of dates for different letters in each reminder you send. When you see that a letter has been submitted, thank them for submitting it and give them a heads up about any other upcoming letters.

NEXT STEPS

The letters of recommendation should be the last step in the process of your application. You're almost done! All that's left is to submit everything. And then . . .? That's actually a tough question. The temptation will be to just sit on pins and needles waiting for news, putting everything else on hold. But that is probably not the best plan. In the final chapter, we'll talk about what happens next and what you can do to help make the next part of the process a little easier.

CALENDAR OF EVENTS FOR AN APPLICATION PROCESS: FALL SEMESTER

This is for an application due in January. Adjust as needed for an earlier due date.

September

Big Goals

1. Talk to professors and advisors and pick schools.
2. Start a draft of your CV and give it to team members to look over.
3. Start planning for the GRE (if needed). When will you take it? How much time is needed to study?

Small Goals

1. Make a check sheet for each school:
    - Due date
    - GRE?
    - Average GPA?
    - Where in USA?
    - What writing do you need to submit? Personal statement, letter of interest, writing sample?

October

Big Goals

1. Start a draft of your CV and give it to team members to look over.
2. Pick a piece of writing to use as your writing sample (if needed). Give it to team members to discuss revisions.
3. Start an outline of your personal statement and share it with team members.
4. Order transcripts (unless you need to have them sent directly to the school, in which case wait until November).

Small Goals

1. Stay in touch with team members.
2. Identify some grad students you can talk to about their experiences applying to grad school and their life in grad school.

November

Big Goals

1. Revise your writing sample.
2. Plan for campus visits, where feasible.
3. Revise your personal statement and share it with your team members.
4. Put together your "About Me" document for those who will be writing you letters of recommendation.
5. Give the "About Me" doc to your team members along with instructions and due dates for your letters.

December

Big Goals

1. Submit your applications!
2. Plan your submissions—you'll have finals, holidays, and a ton of stuff to think about, so you'll need to plan.

PART FOUR

AFTER THE APPLICATION—NOW WHAT?

12

WHAT HAPPENS NEXT

AFTER YOU'VE PERFECTED YOUR LAST DRAFT of every document, pored over every detail, and submitted every application, you get to take a break! Well, kind of. If you are in your last semester of college, you still have classes to pass and a graduation to plan for, and many things will be taking up your attention. Add to all of that the drawn-out pain of waiting to hear back from the programs you've applied to, and your stress may only be rising. After years of working with undergrads, the best advice I can give you is this: Develop a plan for if you get in, and develop another plan for if you don't. Having an idea of what comes next will be a huge help either way. In this chapter, we'll talk about some of the things that happen next, and how you can plan to put yourself in the best position no matter what happens.

HEARING BACK—HOW LONG?

Once you've finally sent in an application, the first thing you'll want to know is when you'll hear back. The truth is that no one can tell you exactly when you'll hear back, which makes this one of the hardest parts of the entire process. While preparing the application, at least there were always things to do—you were moving forward with your future in your hands, actively writing, researching, and managing the process. After you've submitted your last application, all of that is done and there's suddenly a void of time and attention where all that work and forward movement was focused.

The worst thing you can do at this point is let that void sit unfilled, because the most likely things to fill it will be worry and anxiety. You have to keep moving, even though you are in limbo while you wait and that feels a lot like sitting still. Meet with your team, make new plans, fill your time with a new hobby or something, *anything* to distract yourself for the next few months, because it will likely take at least two months, and probably longer, for you to hear back from all your programs.

Most programs tell you that they will let you know in about six to eight weeks, but that is just a guesstimate. Many factors go into determining how long this part of the process takes, and none of them are in your control. Sometimes, departments will be really on the ball and have the whole thing done in four weeks. Other times, there may be all new people on the committee, or a tech failure or some other big issue, and it may take an additional month or two. Unfortunately, in all these situations, there won't be anything you can do.

If you haven't heard back and it's been about the amount of time that the program said they would need before letting you know, feel free to contact the program coordinator to check in on the process. You should be able to get a quick update on where things stand, but don't expect a very exact answer to when you might hear back. The coordinators usually know approximately where the committee is on their timeline, but they often have no power to make that process go faster or to predict exactly when certain things will get done. Remember that if you are contacting the department, the chances are good that other applicants are too, so do your best to be polite and understand that the person you are contacting is likely already under pressure to get things done.

In any case, if you haven't heard back by the time the program initially said they would give you a decision, you must fight the instinct that this is bad news. More likely than not, the delay has no bearing on whether you are going to be accepted or rejected. The delay probably has nothing to do with your application. It's human to assume that if we were going to get in, we would have heard by now, and the fact that we haven't must be a bad sign. The reality is that it's probably only a sign that something else is going on that has nothing to do with you and that you have no control over. Our brains are often hardwired to expect the worst and look for any detail that points toward failure. You must push back against this instinct and try to stay positive. Remember that you are in the middle of running a marathon, not at the end of a sprint. Whether you get in or not, you are going to have to keep running, and if you burn through your energy now on worry and anxiety, you either will have no reserves to keep going when you get a rejection or will enter your new program exhausted and tired.

In the unlikely event that you don't hear back at all, something probably went wrong on their end or on yours. Once you've submitted your application, be in the habit of checking your spam folder *regularly*. I have worked with a couple of students whose acceptance notifications went to their spam folder and they ended up missing their chance to accept. This kind of unforced error hits close to home for me: The offer letter for the job I have now ended up in my spam, and I was extremely lucky that someone called to confirm that I didn't want the job. Since I hadn't responded to their offer, they were ready to move on when one person decided to call me, just to be sure. I almost had a heart attack. Don't let your spam filter screw things up for you—check it regularly.

It's also possible to end up in a weird situation where a school just doesn't get back to you, though this happens far less frequently in the era of online application systems. One thing you can do to help avoid such a glitch is to make sure that you stay on top of your application each step of the way. The online systems should let you track your application and should flag any pieces you still need to turn in, including items like transcripts and letters of recommendation. If ever there is a part of the application package that you're sure you turned in but it is not showing up in the system, call the program contact right away. Putting in a call or an email to note a problem will be a huge help if the issue persists past the due date. If they know that you've been trying to resolve an issue since before the due date, they will be more likely to extend a courtesy of more time to get the issue cleared up. Communication is key throughout the entire process, and this step is no exception.

WHAT IF YOU DON'T GET IN?

This is a tough one to write. Feeling rejected is a deeply personal and painful experience, and with all the work, heart, and energy that a grad school application requires, it can feel like the admission committee gazed directly into your worth as a person and said, "No thanks." I know all too personally how horrible that feels. When I was in the throes of receiving rejection letter after rejection letter, it felt like all the work I had done to get past the rough start to my college career had been for nothing. I had no plan B and no idea what I was going to do next. I had gone "all in" on getting a PhD, and now every place I applied to was telling me I wasn't good enough. At least that's how it felt, and you're likely to take a rejection intensely personally as well, but let me give you a few reasons why it probably isn't personal and some ideas about what you can do next.

It's Never Personal—But It's Always Personal

Let's talk a bit about why this may not be as personal as you think. Although you've poured your heart and soul into your application, for the person on the other end of the computer screen it is just another computer file. We did a lot of work in your personal statements and in your letters of recommendation to help you stand out and break through the noise, but once your application is out of your hands there's not much you can do. There are so many things that can happen after you turn in your application that you won't ever know about. You have no control over the number of other applicants for the program, and you can't control how many of those other applications your reviewer has read before they read your essay. If you are somewhere between number one and number twenty on a given day, your chances of standing out may be pretty good. If you catch some bad luck and your reader has already gone through thirty applications and is eager to start lunch or move on to something else in their day, then no matter how much work you put in, it's going to be an uphill fight to grab their attention.

You also have no control over the mood that your reader is going to be in. Right now, I'm sitting in a quiet room, listening to relaxing music, and I'm able to concentrate and commit myself fully to what I'm doing. In about two hours, my house is going to be full of noisy children. They are children, to be fair, but they are crazy and loud. I'm going to have a twelve-year-old asking for help with his math homework, with a hyperactive eight-year-old bouncing off the walls and playing his music way too loud, not to mention the moody teenager that I will need to convince to walk the dog. Oh, and the dog will be barking. Just thinking about it is stressing me out. If I'm in the process of reading applications and yours hits my screen right now, in my moment of serenity and relaxed focus, you likely have a great shot. But if I'm trying to squeeze in five more applications before the zoo descends on me, good luck. Of course, committees have multiple people reading all the applications, and everyone will do their best to be objective, fair, and consistent. At the same time, these are all just people who may be tired, happy, hopeful, angry, annoyed, or immersed in any part of the human experience you can imagine. We all do our best to take our emotions out of our decision making, but it's not easy.

That dreaded rejection, from one school or from ten, is less about you than you imagine. Our brains are exceptionally good at pointing out our own flaws, and if you get a rejection, your brain will be your own worst enemy for a while, finding and focusing on all the things that could have gone better or should have been different. But the reality is that if you could do the process again, the result would be different. That's why we must prepare to do the process again.

Four years ago, I worked with a shy student who was also funny, smart, and a great writer with straight A's. She didn't have a ton of confidence, though, and when she received five rejection letters, even one from her "safety school," it was devastating. We had a couple of conversations in which I had to talk her back from the edge. She was convinced that there was some big piece missing from her application that would have made all the difference. A few months later, though, she had picked herself up, set her sights on what came next, and met me to talk about her applications for the following year. Not much changed from one application cycle to the next. Her great GPA was almost the same as when she had applied before, and the same people wrote her letters of recommendation. But this time around, she was accepted to five out of six schools, including three that had rejected her the first time. Her application hadn't changed much, but she had stayed persistent and kept pushing. It paid off.

So, if I've done my job and convinced you that you may not actually be an irredeemably bad college student who will never be accepted, what should you do between now and when it's time to apply again? Even though a rejection is not necessarily a reflection of you and what you are capable of, there are things you can do in the meantime that might help your odds the next time around.

Making a Plan

The first temptation will be to focus solely on your application and what you can change for next time. That's not a bad idea, and we will go over things that you can do in that direction, but the biggest thing to think about now is how you will set up your life for the next eight to ten months so that you will be in a good position to apply again. Even though the time between now and when you apply next seems like forever, it will go by fast. If you are finishing your undergrad degree, you still have your last semester to finish, along with graduation and all the family functions and celebrations. Summer will come as it always does, and not much will feel different until the fall, but by then the college semester will have started and, hopefully, you're back in touch with your team and back at work on your application.

The biggest issue is finding a way to allow yourself to be persistent. We often think about persistence as a personality trait. But it is as much about setting your world up in a way that allows for persistence as it is about anything buried in your DNA. In other words, your life circumstances play a huge role in giving you the time and opportunities to keep applying, keep working, keep pushing. If you plan now, it will be much easier to take on the applications again in a few months.

The two big pressing issues to think through are living arrangements and work. Obviously, this will be easier for some new graduates than for others. If you already have a family and a job, your living and work situation may not change much, but if you work on campus or have been living in the dorms throughout college, some big moves are likely coming up. If you can start to think ahead to the coming year and planning for these realities, you'll be more prepared when it comes time to start in on applications again. Many of you may not know where you're going to work in the coming months but are planning to look for a new job once you graduate. That makes total sense and is a great idea, but don't lose sight of the amount of time you are going to need to devote to applications in the future. Now is a great time to start working on a schedule that will give you practice setting aside blocks of time for the project, especially in the fall, when you are going to need to be more disciplined about when you get work done, especially if you have a full-time job.

After-Application Analysis with Your Team

The first thing to do, if you find out you didn't get into the schools you applied to, is *talk to your team*. Your first instinct will be to curl up in a ball and hide. I know because that's how I felt. It's a natural reaction to feeling embarrassed and disappointed. Talking about it means thinking about it again, going over it again in your head, and opening yourself up again to the feelings of rejection. No one wants to do that, so a common first reaction is to just keep quiet. This is a bad reaction, and it's the worst thing to do if your goal is to eventually end up in a graduate program. We here on the other side of the desk are not going to be disappointed in you or think less of you if you didn't get in. We've written enough letters and worked with enough students to know how this whole thing works, and we know that the game is often rigged from the start. If you talk to us, there are ways we can help; if you hide, there is nothing we can do. I've had so many students over the years who asked for letters of recommendation and then disappeared off the face of the earth for months at a time. Eventually, I would get happy news when I happened to see them in the halls of the university—they let me know they got in and were now attending classes. But I hadn't heard from them for six months, a year, or even several years later—they were silently working up the courage to try again. The number one thing that meeting with your team can help with is pushing back against the feeling that all is lost and that your goal of a graduate degree is over. We can help with a lot more, but the best thing a good team can provide in this situation is hope. We're experienced and know that there is hope to be found.

When you find time to sit down with your team again, the first thing you should talk about—after a few tears and a few choice curse words for the admission committees that screwed you over—is a plan for what comes next.

WHAT TO CONSIDER FOR NEXT TIME

Big Picture

Think about the programs you applied to and why you chose them. It's easy to develop tunnel vision in that regard, as the momentum and looming deadlines of applications don't allow the time to pull back and rethink your choices. You do have that time now, though, and it's a great idea to revisit your reasons for applying to those programs. Has anything changed about your goals or career aspirations since you sent in your applications? Spend some time talking through those goals with your team. During your first application cycle, when you were busy writing your statement and tracking down people to be on your team and write your letters, you may not have taken the time to talk with them about *why* you wanted to apply to these particular programs, to see whether they had any insights into the programs and your career path that might have influenced your choices. Now is a really good time to have those conversations.

Even if you are dead-set on the direction you want to go in, you can always talk with your team, your university career center, and other people in the field itself about other career options you may not have been exposed to. You don't need to give up on your dream, but stay open to learning about options you haven't considered. Knowing about these alternatives may not change your mind at all, or it may make you more positive than ever that you picked the right area, but both of those outcomes are good things. The best situation is that you go into a grad program and into a career field fully aware of the alternatives and of why you decided to go in the direction you did. This greatly reduces the possibility that you will learn, later on, of some option that, if you had just known about it sooner, you might have picked instead. There is no guarantee that you will never find yourself thinking, "If only I had known . . . ," but the more time you put into research and to communicating with your team, the less likely this becomes.

SCHOOLS Researching the full range of possible schools and programs is another area that people often shortchange because of time pressure. Later, many will realize that they didn't really spend enough time researching the options. This is especially relevant if you've recently thought more about your goals and identified other career or grad school areas you might want to explore. New career options mean new graduate degree options, which means that schools you hadn't considered before may be on the table. Now that you don't have the pressure of a deadline looming, you can do your research in a more relaxed situation. You might consider visiting the campuses of universities you're now considering, to see if the programs you're interested in offer information sessions or if people in the department are willing to meet with you.

APPLICATION MATERIALS Keep your team in the loop as you reevaluate and update your application materials. There will probably be at least one area in your application that didn't get as much attention as it needed in the first round and could use another few drafts. Now is a great time to identify those areas and start making plans for improving your current application packet.

EXPERIENCE This is an area that comes up often in application conversations. Many students feel that the programs they are applying to expect them to have more experience than they currently have. We talked about this a bit in regard to the personal statement section—

what counts as experience? If your application is missing something, such as volunteer experience or internship hours, that you just didn't have time for previously, you could brainstorm ways to take on an internship over the next few months or, even better, look for a job in a field related to the programs you're applying to. This is the most time-intensive intervention I've suggested, so be sure to consult your team about the pluses and minuses of taking on a commitment like a job or an internship, to be sure it's absolutely needed.

CV This is probably the document that people spend the least amount of time on in their application package, but now is a great time to devote a little more attention to it. If you haven't made a trip to your university's career or writing center to go over your CV, do it now. The CV is not a big deciding factor in your application package, but a good CV can add to a strong package and a sloppy-looking one can detract, so focusing on the visual element as well as the content is a good idea.

GPA WORK This could range from relatively easy to relatively intense, depending on what needs to be done. If you have some F's on your transcripts that you didn't have a chance to remove earlier, now is the time. Look back at chapter 7 to see if any of the strategies for improving your GPA fit your situation. The academic renewal or credit/no credit options are the easiest, but it will be more time consuming if you need to take additional classes. If you are considering extra classes, be sure to talk with your team first to make sure they are really needed. GPA is important, but before you spend time and money on raising it, you should get a few insights into whether this is the way to go.

TEST SCORES If you had to take a test for your application, there is the possibility that a higher score will help your application. Remember that scores are just numbers, but in some circumstances a score will mean the difference between your carefully prepared application materials being read or being discarded. If your original score met the minimum for your application to be considered, I think that there is a real conversation to be had with your team about whether it is worth the time and effort to retake the test.

PERSONAL STATEMENT How many drafts did your personal statement go through, and how many of those drafts did you get feedback on? If the answer to either question is one or two, there is probably room to improve your personal statement. During your first application cycle, there was a ton of pressure and it was difficult to know how to divide your time. That will be less of an issue now and you can really focus on the things that matter most. If your personal statement was one of the pieces that got sidetracked during the first cycle, now is the time to give it more attention. Now, with the benefit of more time, you can meet with team members to go through your statement paragraph by paragraph and talk about what you should keep and what can be changed. The reduced time pressure hopefully means less stress, and you can work on the statement with renewed focus.

WHAT IF YOU GET IN?

Can You Say No?

You've done all the hard work. You've put in the time, the energy, and the money. And now you've been accepted to a program. However, something has changed. Maybe you were also accepted into another program that you are more excited by, or life has thrown an unexpected obstacle in your way and now the school you were accepted to is no longer a good option.

This happens more often than you think. If you apply to multiple schools, there's a decent chance some variation will happen to you. What to do? First things first: You need to know that *an application or even an acceptance of admission is not a contract.* You are not legally bound to attend any of the universities or programs you applied to, even if they offer you admission and you accept. You can always change your mind. Even if you start attending classes, there is almost always a drop date—if you withdraw from a class or even from the university before that date, your tuition can be refunded or financial aid can be reimbursed. This is something that happens every semester, for both grad students and undergrads alike.

When you are accepted into a program, they will most likely give you a date by which they want you to accept admission. If it is a particularly competitive program, they may not give you any more than a week to accept or decline. In those cases, there is almost never any downside to accepting an admission. Even if you still have an open application that you are waiting to hear back about, you can always withdraw this acceptance later if you get accepted by a school you're more interested in attending. For the most part, there is no downside to accepting admission into a program, even if you're not sure that you will attend that university in the fall.

Please understand, though, that if you accept, someone else down the list is going to get a "no" or get put on a waiting list. If you know that there is absolutely no way you will actually attend, say no. If you accept and then decide you won't be attending, let the program know *as soon as possible.* The sooner you let them know, the better the chance there will still be time for someone else to be accepted and attend. Be sure to think about the situation both from the perspective of someone who is accepted and from that of someone who is wait-listed. If you end up on the waiting list, you will be thanking God for the angel who turned down admission and cleared a spot for you. If you get accepted and know you can't make it, do everything you can to be that angel for another person.

You might also consider delaying your admission. Many universities provide the option of setting aside your admission for one year for whatever reason, allowing you to finish what you need to in the meantime and start attending the following fall. Not every university offers this, and being granted a delay may not be an automatic thing, but the option is usually there if something prevents you from starting right away. If this applies to you, the sooner you talk to the department about it, the better.

In the big picture, programs know that not all the students they offer spots to are going to accept. Having a student accept and then withdraw is something that happens every year, so don't stress out too much about it. Given that the odds are often against us, we need to be smart about our choices. The smart thing to do here is to accept an offer if you get one. If a better option becomes available later, let the original department know, politely and quickly, and then accept the better offer.

Grad School with Family and Kids

Many of you are seniors in college and haven't had a chance to do much besides being a student and probably working a job on or off campus. But there are many students who have lived a lot of life outside of college and are considering going into graduate school with more responsibilities than other students. When I first started graduate school, I had just gotten married that summer, and by the start of my second year, our first baby was on the way. By the time I finished the PhD program, I had two kids, a wife with a professional job, and all kinds of responsibilities outside of what I did as a student.

If this sounds like you, there are things to consider about grad school and how you can make it work with the life you already have. Whether it's work, family, or other considerations, many of us don't have the ability to choose a life arranged solely around what's happening on campus. There are some downsides to having outside responsibilities, but there are also a lot of upsides that we should talk about as well.

Downsides and How to Deal with Them

These should be obvious. The more demands there are on your time, the less time you have to devote to school and the more critical it is to schedule your time. If you've gone through your undergraduate education with these same constraints, hopefully you've developed a system by now. If you haven't, now is a great time to start. One important thing to realize is that family and work responsibilities will expand to fill any free space you give them. If your time management plan is to postpone doing your schoolwork until you have free time, you are going to have some problems—because your home and your job are basically going to conspire to make sure you never have any. As I sit at home right now, the dog needs to be walked, there are dishes to be done, laundry to wash, I need to plan dinner, not to mention a thousand other small things that need to happen around the house. If you let them, the million little tasks will eat up your day, your week, and any other amount of time you give them. The solution is to schedule time for your application project, block it off just like you would time for work, and be protective of anything encroaching on that time. What you end up doing in that time is up to you. Hopefully, you find ways to use it productively, but if you don't make sure to set it aside and protect it, everything else around you will grow to fill in the void.

Another downside of having outside responsibilities is not having time for all the benefits and opportunities grad school can offer. In addition to what happens in the classroom, there are a ton of possibilities to take advantage of on campus—going to talks, attending events put on by your department or college, finding new scholarship or grant opportunities to apply for, and networking with others in your classes. These connections can make a huge difference when it comes time to find a job or to get inside information about classes or opportunities. The downside here is that when you have a lot of responsibilities outside of school, there can be very little time to take advantage of any of these. Remember that as first-generation college students, part of our job is to build the networks that other people may already have by virtue of their parents and their extended family. As a first-gen student, you likely don't have networks to provide the kind of information and opportunities you are going to need to take full advantage of your degree. The solution here is to be extremely proactive about identifying such opportunities as far in advance as possible and making them part of your schedule as soon as possible. As an undergrad, you probably trained yourself to ignore the fifty daily emails you received from the university about all kinds of things that didn't apply to you. However, somewhere in those fifty were probably two or three that did apply, and since you didn't see them, you won't know to set aside time for the event or to take advantage of an opportunity. As a grad student, getting good at staying on top of your campus announcements, skimming past the ones that don't apply, and finding the ones that do will be a hugely valuable skill. If you just delete or dismiss these announcements out of hand, you are going to be missing out on a lot, and the sooner you know about them, the sooner you can set aside the time on your calendar.

Finding time to network can also be tricky for someone with a family, especially when it comes to networking with your classmates. Getting together with people outside of class doesn't always happen on a schedule. If you can, though, try to set up a few regular times to meet with people outside of class. A coffee or lunch every two weeks with several people from your classes, or a regular online meeting where you can all share info and vent about what's happening in your program, will help you keep in touch on a schedule. Not all the other students will have a restrictive schedule, so you may need to be the one to initiate these types of meetings, but it will be worth it. The information and support you get from your peers can make the difference between just barely scraping by and thriving in a program.

The Upsides

There are some amazing upsides to going into a grad program with a family, especially if you communicate with them about what you need and how they can help. The biggest upside is that you have a built-in support system that you can lean on when things get rough. Family will play a huge role in helping lay the groundwork for all the things you will need to do in graduate school, but they won't know what you need automatically. You have to communicate to them the types of things you're going to need as you go through the program. Obviously, those include time—time to study, time to go to classes, time to work. But more time spent in your program means less time available for things you would normally do as part of the family. It's easy to account for the fact that you'll need more time, but if you forget to plan for how to cover all the things you would normally handle around the house, there will be trouble quick.

The advantage of having a built-in support system can be enormous. Grad school can often be competitive and anxiety inducing, with constant exposure to the possibility of being judged by others. Fun! This environment is going to be rough on everyone, but if you have a group of people at home who support you no matter what, you have a solid base to build from. Having a family at home often meant that I was not as connected to or invested in some of the personal drama and day-to-day issues that can come to define life as a graduate student. For me, that wasn't a bad thing at all. There is enough to fill your time and attention without having to stress about gossip or rumors. Having a group of people you are connected to, who are outside of that system, will be a way to get some distance and keep some perspective.

CAN YOU WORK WHILE IN GRAD SCHOOL?

Most of the first-generation students I know have had jobs throughout their undergraduate years. I was the same way. Financial aid sometimes helped with tuition and books, but it was never enough to live on. My parents couldn't really help with that either, so working while I was in school was never really a question—it was just a reality. When I speak to students who are planning to go to graduate school, this can be a big point of worry. They found a way to make their undergraduate program work while holding down a job, but will that be different at the graduate school level? Most of us have heard horror stories about the workload in graduate programs, and it's a real concern that if the amount of work increases, there may be less time for a job. If your rent and your food depend on you maintaining a job, working less may not be an option, so what do you do?

Is It Possible?

The short answer is that yes, it is possible to have a job while you are a graduate student. Whether it's a good idea is another question altogether. Many master's programs are built around the idea that students are likely going to be working and will need to have some flexibility in their schedule. You can get a sense of whether the program you are applying to accounts for this by looking at the class schedules. Are there night class options or hybrid options for some of the courses? Are the classes offered only during the day and spread across all five weekdays? Looking at the way their classes are timed and the days they are offered can provide a good insight into whether the professors in a program expect their students to be working. Not all programs are going to be built with working students in mind. Many take the attitude that students have to make their lives fit around the program and the department, and that offering and accounting for outside work is not their problem. Knowing what type of department you're going into can be a big help in terms of trying to plan out your time and availability.

The type of work you do is also a big consideration. If you have an on-campus job that offers some forms of flexibility and enough downtime that you can do some classwork or reading while you are on the clock, it may be relatively easy to make that job work with your classes. But if your job requires a lot of physical work that can wear you out, and includes no downtime for doing homework, it's going to be a lot more difficult.

This is another time in the overall process when you will have to ask some introspective questions. What is your energy level? If your job is already demanding a lot of energy, will you have enough left to take on a demanding program? What type of environments do you need to do good work? Your job may let you get in some reading every now and then, but are you going to be interrupted constantly, making it hard to concentrate? Overall, you need to be as honest as possible with yourself and make a realistic assessment of how much time you are going to have to devote to schoolwork, while still being able to pay the bills. The harsh reality is that if, at some point, your choices come down to turning in a paper or earning enough money to pay rent, most likely your job is going to win out over school. Better to think hard about those circumstances now, rather than when you find yourself in a tight spot later.

All of this is really planning for the harder cases. In many instances, people have flexible jobs that allow them to devote enough time to an academic program. If your employers have already been supportive of you as an undergraduate, hopefully they will remain so during your graduate program. But no matter how understanding your employer may be, it is important to plan scenarios where they may not be so understanding. An economic downturn, a loss of business, or the loss of other employees can turn even a great work environment into a stressful one.

Practical Considerations

I don't know exactly what the workload will like be in the program you are interested in. While I wish I could tell you that you'll be fine, the reality is that while some grad programs require a similar amount of work as your undergrad program, others require significantly more. The only way to get any idea is to do some research on the programs. I talked about grad handbooks in chapter 6. These can be a great place to get an idea of what your course load will be like each semester. You can also email department coordinators, department chairs, or other professors to ask for a copy of the syllabus for a class you plan to take. Those should give you some idea of the type and amount of work you will be expected to do in each class. This is another good time for a self-inventory. What types of classwork and what types of testing are going to be the most challenging for you? Essay writing is extremely taxing for some students, while tests bring more stress to others. Examining the syllabus and talking to the professor can give you a much clearer idea of the work you'll be facing in your first semester, and then you can make more informed decisions and better plans based on a realistic time commitment for classes. Between the grad handbook, class schedules from the year before, and a set of syllabi, you should have a pretty good idea what your first semester is going to look like. Hopefully, you can use that knowledge to effectively fit the coursework in with your job.

PhD Programs

The work/school time equation is a little different if you are in a PhD program, sometimes for the better, sometimes for the worse. Most PhD programs view your studies as your job, and they are not going to be built around the idea that students have outside commitments, even if many of their students depend on outside work to get by. Academics can be myopic in this respect. You have to remember that your professors likely became professors because they were extremely good at school, and, in all likelihood, many of them have never really held private-sector jobs outside the academic world. That can make them a little shortsighted when it comes to the reality of their students' lives. The basic viewpoint of most PhD programs is that this is a process to train you to become an academic, with the expectation that your life and career will *be* academic work, and therefore you need to make academic work your life and career as a grad student. That doesn't mean that you can't fit a job into the equation, but big issues will likely arise if you have to maintain significant employment outside of the college. Again, most PhD programs are not set up with working students in mind. Expect that classes will be at all times of day and likely across the five days of the week. On top of that, meetings with advisors will likely need to be during normal working hours on weekdays, and many department functions and events will be during those times as well.

Because PhD programs are expecting you to make academic work your life, many of the activities, talks, lectures, and other informal meetings that make up being a PhD student can be a huge part of your development and success in the program. That includes your own work on your dissertation topic, which is supposed to be taking place outside and beyond class assignments and TA work. If we really break down the time expectations in a PhD program, it's a ratio of work-hours as a TA, the work you're assigned in your classes, and the work you're expected to do on your own research. Those three commitments together can easily fill a forty-hour workweek, and often the expectation is that you are working well beyond those hours to make progress on your dissertation.

This doesn't make outside work impossible. I found ways to make outside work a part of my PhD program pretty much the entire time I was a graduate student. However, that ended up costing me in some important ways. The fact that I had a major time commitment outside of my department and my research meant that I was sometimes behind my peers in developing my research. I could keep up with coursework, but I found myself falling behind on things that didn't have a strict deadline attached to them.

Time management can become an issue in any program, PhD or not, but it seems to be particularly common in programs and departments that expect the program to basically be your life. This is part of the reality for first-gen students, who have to get used to navigating spaces where others have more time and money than we do.

NOW WHAT?

Whether you are planning to apply again or planning to start your new program in the fall, it's likely you'll soon be stepping into the unknown. You may be a newly accepted grad student, or adjusting to a life without the title of "student" for the first time since you started kindergarten—either way, this next part is going to be a challenge. In the conclusion, I'll talk a little about the mindset to take into this new part of your life and how to plan for it.

CONCLUSION

MY WRITING ADVENTURE

I told you at the beginning of this book that I was rejected by eight different graduate programs the first year I applied. It was crushing. Let me tell you about something else that was crushing, and much more recent: I erased several months' worth of work on this book by accident and there was no way to get it back. I had been granted a sabbatical by my university for the following fall semester, to write this book. Even though the sabbatical wouldn't begin until September, I was all wound up by January, wanting to start work on the project as soon as possible. I was worried about the process of writing, self-conscious about my writing style, and aware that I hadn't written anything academic in a few years. COVID and all the craziness that came with it basically meant that teaching and being a husband and dad was about all I had recently had energy for. Starting a new project was intimidating. I wasn't sure where to begin, I wasn't sure what the process was going to be like, and all of that uncertainty added up to anxiety. I didn't want to waste my sabbatical time and end up with nothing to show for it. I felt guilty that I was being granted what was essentially a four-month vacation just to write, and I wasn't even sure how I was going to pull it off.

Over the months leading up to the sabbatical, I plotted and planned, took notes, made outlines, and wrote rough drafts of a few sections. Over the summer, I wrote a few more pieces. Now I was feeling good. My kids went back to school, and on the first day of my actual sabbatical, I biked ten miles to a coffee shop with my laptop to officially begin my long writing project. I opened the laptop, tried to open my notes, outlines, and drafts, and they were all gone. Everything. My stomach dropped and I started to feel panic setting in. I'm decently technical, so I started trying every tech tip and trick I knew to find the files. It was no use. They were all gone.

That afternoon, after biking ten miles back home in the Sacramento heat, feeling like I was going to throw up the entire time, I had a decision to make: allow this to completely throw me off track and kill my project, or start over. Start all the way over, from nothing. The book that you are reading is, in many ways, a second draft that is the result of my starting over in the middle of August 2024, redoing everything I had already done and then pushing past that to write the rest. As I'm writing now, I have close to eighty thousand words and the makings of an actual book. Not bad for a guy who used to work at Taco Bell.

I'm telling this story because, like you, I have had to step into the unknown at several points in my life. And there have been several times when that bravery has been met with failure and rejection (often my own fault, though not always). This book is an actual, published and printed book sitting in your hands now, even though, as I'm writing this now in my living room, it's already been rejected by fifteen publishers. The number would be higher, but quite a few of them haven't even bothered to respond to my emails. We don't have a choice about the fact that we are most likely going to fail at some point and be asked to start over. The question is always what we will do after that happens. The goal of getting into graduate school and getting a graduate degree is a huge one. It can seem impossible, and for the most part we have no idea about what the process will be like, the challenges we are going to face, and what new opportunities we might have when we finish. All of this can be enormously stressful, and if we don't take the time to consider how we approach this project, the stress or indecision can cause further problems.

The idea here is that we need to think about the *mindset* we bring to this project as a whole, and make sure we're thinking about it in a way that sets us up to succeed in the long run. The concept of mindset gets overused and misused. Despite what you may have seen on YouTube, mindset is not a magical practice that will gain you health, wealth, and a model spouse. Mindset is actually the practice of thinking about how you approach the world around you and being aware of the ways your attitude influences your perceptions of both the opportunities and the setbacks you will encounter. For the project that we are taking on, rejection is a big possibility throughout. We are putting ourselves out into the world, and there is a decent chance that our efforts will be met with rejection and negative feedback. We're also trying to do something that is new and untested in our experience: to access and operate in spaces that we have no personal precedent for and no solid knowledge about.

From our perspective as outsiders to a system we are trying to access, it makes a lot of sense that all of our planning and efforts are hyperfocused on getting through the door. There are some problems with this mindset, though. Many of the students I work with can be so focused on getting through the door that they forget to ask whether the door they are focusing on is the right one for them, whether what awaits them on the other side is a good fit for who they are and what they want to do. The other problem with focusing so much on getting in is that you are setting yourself up for a big energy dump when you *do* get in.

For example, when I was rejected by all the schools I first applied to, I put an enormous amount of time, energy, and attention into getting into a program the next time around. Of course, this is a natural reaction to rejection, and in a lot of ways it paid off to be hyper-focused on what I could do to get a different result. On the other hand, being so fixated on getting in meant that I often overlooked my mental and physical well-being, burning myself out to produce the best possible application. When I was finally accepted, it brought a huge feeling of accomplishment, but also a huge feeling of relief. I had put so much effort and mental energy into this particular outcome that once it was here, my whole body basically said, "Thank God that's over!"—and immediately started to collapse. I had focused so much effort on getting in that when fall semester came around, instead of being energized, fresh, and ready to take on this new challenge, I was nearly completely burned out. This caused some issues. My mental and physical energy just wasn't where I needed it to be when I started the new program, and it was a struggle to get myself back into the right shape to give my all.

Recalling that experience, and drawing on more than a decade working with hundreds of undergraduates, I think that the better mindset to have going into this project is that *you are going to get in eventually and you need to plan for that reality.* The application process is brutal, but it is temporary. When you eventually do get in, you are going to have to deal with a new reality: The application was just the first step up the side of a whole new mountain to climb. If you can start with the mindset that this application process is temporary, and that you need to devote time and thought to both what you are going to do after you get in, after you graduate, *and* what you can do to help preserve your energy and your sanity right now, you'll be in much better shape in the long run.

I realize that in giving you this advice, I am being somewhat hypocritical. Yes, I was able to deal with a big blow when my work on this book got deleted, by moving forward to keep pushing on this project.

After bouncing back from that disaster, though, I had a rough time dealing with rejection from publishers. It's easier said than done, keeping a positive attitude and focusing on the bigger picture. But often that's what advice is: lessons from people who would do things differently the second time around, who, with the benefit of hindsight, can see where they took a wrong turn. I don't give any of the advice in this book with the idea that following it will be easy. I think that even if I'd had a good guide when I was in my mid-twenties and applying to graduate schools, I would still have had a rough time planning, not waiting until the last minute, and putting myself out there to talk to the people I needed to. I would still have been afraid of rejection, worried about making the wrong impression, and way too critical of my own abilities. I give this advice because I know the things I struggled with, and because I've seen so many people struggling with very similar issues. Being a trailblazer is not easy, but luckily, even though you may be the first person in your family to go to college, you aren't the first person *ever* to get here from similar circumstances, and there are many of us who will be willing to help you along the way. Talk to us, even though you're afraid and intimidated. Get help. No one does this alone.

IT'S ALWAYS PERSONAL, BUT IT'S NOT PERSONAL (AGAIN)

In a class I teach every year that covers classic sociological theory, I do an exercise with the students that always seems to get interesting results. I ask them to tell me why they aren't going to Harvard instead of our small state college in the middle of California's Central Valley. I like our college, we do a great job, and our students get a great education, but if someone has the choice, they should absolutely go to Harvard. Across the board, a person who attends Harvard will have many more opportunities in life. Opportunities in terms of jobs, in terms of health and well-being, in terms of quality of life. There is no denying that your life chances are just a lot better if you attend Harvard. So why aren't my students there instead?

The answers I get are pretty similar each year. The first is always that it's too expensive. This is true—Harvard can be enormously expensive—but very few students I've asked have ever actually looked up how much it costs to go to Harvard or what they might receive in financial aid if they went. The second most frequent answer is that they didn't have good enough grades. This is probably true too. Harvard and other Ivy League universities are extremely exclusive and can have intense GPA and testing requirements (strangely, though, while neither George W. Bush nor Donald Trump was known for his academic success, both managed to get into Ivy League universities). Here, too, when I ask students what grades or test scores they would need in order to get into Harvard, they have no idea.

Even though I've been teaching for close to fifteen years, and I've been running this mini-experiment each year, I have only ever had, at most, five students who had seriously considered going to Harvard and had done the research. Even though I've had thousands of students in my classes, none of them had ever actually applied. Why not? Even if a student thought they had an almost zero chance of getting in, wouldn't it at least be worth a complete "shot in the dark" application if it meant they might get a chance to change their life forever?

The reality is that it's completely unfair for me to ask this question. My students and I both know the real reason they didn't apply. At some point in their lives, they had received the message—from TV, from movies, from friends and family, from *somewhere*—that Harvard was not a place for people like them. Unfortunately, that idea is completely correct. When we look at the breakdown of Harvard's student body, less than 5 percent of students come from the bottom 20 percent of the income distribution. Using data from the "Equality of Opportunity" study, *Harvard Magazine* found that the number of students from the top 0.1 percent of the income scale who attend the university equals the number of students from the bottom 20 percent who attend. In fact, the magazine reported that the number of Harvard students who come from the top 0.1 percent had been growing over the decade prior to the report. Instead of getting better, the situation was getting worse: Harvard was becoming even more elitist.

Here's the problem. When I talk to my students about why they aren't at Harvard, they almost always interpret not being "Harvard material" as a *personal failing*. At some point, each had decided individually that they were not smart enough, not hardworking enough, not outstanding enough to even be considered for admission to an elite university like Harvard. Almost none of them had arrived at the correct conclusion about the situation: It's not that they are not smart enough, it's that they are not *rich* enough.

I bring up this example because, when I look back at my own experiences as a first-generation college student and think about all the other first-gen students I've worked with over the years, this story comes to mind again and again. Bright, talented, and outstanding students have trouble accessing institutions and opportunities that they are perfectly well qualified for. It's due not to a lack of effort or intelligence, but to a lack of *information and connections*, both of which are often the direct result of the student's own economic status. Inevitably, when first-generation students encounter these obstacles, they see the problem as a *personal failing* rather than as a *system that was not built with them in mind*.

After years of teaching first-gen students, I am completely confident in saying that you are just as capable, just as intelligent, just as full of potential and talent as anyone I've ever encountered in my many years of higher education. The people who go to Harvard and Yale, the people who go to graduate school, who become lawyers or doctors, psychologists or pharmacists, aren't somehow magically smarter than you, or in possession of some secret work ethic you don't have. Instead, what they had was *opportunity*, *information*, and *resources*. Without those three in hand, trying to access systems of higher education can be like trying to teach yourself to play piano. Could you do it? Maybe, but it's probably going to take a lot longer and be enormously more frustrating than if you just had access to a piano teacher and could afford some lessons. Most people in this situation will just give up.

Graduate school can be a gateway to better job opportunities, better circumstances, and overall better quality of life. But getting access to those institutions can be shrouded in mystery and misinformation. If we don't have people who have gone this way before to show us the path, things are going to be a lot harder. My hope for any of you reading this book is that it makes your journey a little easier. I hope that with more information and more insight, accessing these institutions is a little less intimidating. I've worked with enough first-generation students to know that once they get the knowledge and the opportunity, they are likely to share it with others, to pass it on, to be a guide. If the information in this book is helpful to you, share it, pass it on, be a guide for others around you. Our communities and our families have often sacrificed enormously for us to go to college and earn a degree. The way we pay them back is not just by moving up in the world; it's also by holding the door open behind us. We pay them back by showing others how to access the systems we did and making their journey a little easier. Colleges and universities were not built with people like us in mind, but they fucked up. They let us in. Now that we're here, our job is to keep the party going and bring as many people as we can along with us. It's not an easy task, and it can be frightening to be the first to do anything. But if you're first-generation, you've made a life out of stepping out into the unknown. One more time won't kill you.

EPILOGUE

Where to Go for More Information

I'VE SAID MANY TIMES over the course of this book that you should not rely on any one source of information, *even this book*. You need to get as many insights into the process as you can. I am going to list some books here that have influenced me in my own thinking about graduate school and how to access it, as well as about the larger world around us. None of these books has all the answers, and not all of them are directly about graduate school. But this is a set of books that I think can be useful to you as you make your way through the process. I've found some inspiration here, and I hope you will too.

Is Grad School for Me? Demystifying the Application Process for First-Gen BIPOC Students
Yvette Martínez-Vu and Miroslava Chavez-Garcia
University of California Press, 2024

This is an excellent book, especially for people who are considering PhDs. The authors do a great job walking you through the process of applying and talking about what life may be like in a grad program. The book is mostly about applying to and being in a PhD program, but there is great information in there for everyone, and I would absolutely recommend this as a second resource to compare with the ideas and advice in this book.

A Field Guide to Grad School: Uncovering the Hidden Curriculum
Jessica Calarco
Princeton University Press, 2020

This is a great book for people considering a PhD program. It explains the application process, provides extensive information on planning out your time in a program, and lays out the steps you'll need to take along the way. If you are seriously considering a PhD, and even if you've been accepted and are getting ready to start, there will be something for you in this book.

The Latinx Guide to Graduate School
Genevieve Negrón-Gonzales and Magdalena L. Barrera
Duke University Press, 2023

This is a fantastic book for anyone, especially but not only Latinx people. All first-gen students will find something useful here while they are thinking about their grad school career. The book is more focused on how life will be once you are in a program and less about the application process itself. But as I've said previously, you need to plan for *when* you get in, not *if* you get in. From that perspective, this book provides an enormous amount of information that can help ensure your success in grad school. It has a particularly good section about planning for your future and how grad school may fit into that picture.

Grad School Essentials: A Crash Course in Scholarly Skills
Zachary Shore
University of California Press, 2016

Applying and getting into a grad program is a huge task, but the ride doesn't stop there, and you will need to be prepared for the work you will do in grad school and beyond. This book is a great primer for that, full of useful tips and insider advice. Everyone will find something valuable here.

Teaching to Transgress: Education as the Practice of Freedom
bell hooks
Routledge Press, 1994

This book is largely aimed toward teachers, but almost all of us as first-gen students are going to be teachers in one sense of the word or another—if not as a profession, then as a matter of survival and a matter of community, passing down what we learn to the next generation. For that reason, this book can be a great source of inspiration and comfort.

Critical Race Counterstories Along the Chicana/Chicano Educational Pipeline
Tara J. Yosso
Routledge Press, 2006

Everyone, whether Chicana/o or not, will find some part of their educational story in this book, especially if they are first-generation. Hearing stories of struggle, triumph, and failure from others' perspectives, seeing the obstacles they face and how they confront them, can be critical to keeping ourselves grounded, focused, and ready to fight. *All* of us as working-class people are part of a "counterstory"—a story of oppression and resistance by people at the margins of society.

A People's History of the United States
Howard Zinn
Harper Perennial Modern Classics, 2015

Here's another book that's not directly about graduate school. But if you are a first-generation student in the United States and you want to know the history that laid the groundwork for you to be here—not the whitewashed, fanciful version of history that we so often get in our classes, but a real history of struggle and of everyday people like you and me—start here.

Glossary of Graduate School Terms

ACADEMIC RENEWAL: A program offered by some colleges that allows students to apply to have low grades, such as F's, removed from their academic record after a certain amount of time has passed.

ACADEMIC WORLD: The environment of universities, colleges, and research institutions.

ADJUNCT FACULTY: A part-time professor hired on a contingent, per-course basis, who typically receives fewer benefits and less job security than tenure-track faculty.

APPLICATION FEES: A fee you must pay to a university for processing your application, which can range from $60 to more than $125 per application.

BURNOUT: A state of emotional exhaustion resulting from prolonged stress, often experienced by students as a result of academic demands.

COMMUNITY SUPPORT: The idea that students who succeed should help others by sharing knowledge, offering guidance, and advocating equitable access to educational opportunities.

CREDENTIAL PROGRAM: A specialized, non-degree program that provides the necessary certification or qualifications to work in a specific field, such as teaching.

CV (CURRICULUM VITAE): A detailed document summarizing a person's academic and professional history, including education, work experience, skills, and achievements. It is more detailed than a résumé and is commonly used in academic settings.

DISSERTATION: A long research paper, the culmination of a PhD program, that presents the student's original research and findings.

FEE WAIVER: A program that allows you to apply to a graduate school without paying the application fee. These are sometimes available to students receiving a federal Pell Grant and may be on a first come, first served basis.

FIRST-GENERATION STUDENT: A student whose parents did not complete a four-year college degree.

GATEKEEPING: The process by which certain groups are included or excluded from opportunities in education or other fields.

GRADUATE COORDINATOR: A person within a university department who manages the administrative aspects of a graduate program and provides information to prospective students.

GRADUATE HANDBOOK: A document that outlines all the requirements, policies, and timelines for a specific graduate program. It is the graduate-level equivalent of an undergraduate catalog.

GRE (GRADUATE RECORD EXAMINATIONS): A standardized test often required for admission to graduate programs, which costs $220 (though a fee reduction program is available).

IMPACTED PROGRAM: A program, often at a public university, that receives a high number of applications for a limited number of spots, making it difficult for students to get in.

INTERNSHIP: A short period during which a student or trainee works at an establishment to gain practical work experience and on-the-job training.

LETTERS OF RECOMMENDATION: Documents submitted by professors, advisors, or professionals who vouch for an applicant's qualifications and character.

LOWER-DIVISION REQUIREMENTS: Basic courses usually taken early in an undergraduate program to fulfill general education requirements.

MAJOR CLASSES: Courses taken in the student's primary field of study, which are required to earn a degree in that subject.

MASTER'S DEGREE: An advanced academic degree pursued after a bachelor's degree that typically focuses on providing advanced knowledge and skills for a specific career path.

MASTER'S THESIS: A lengthy research paper or project required for many master's degrees that demonstrates a student's competence in a field and is typically shorter than a dissertation.

NO CREDIT (NC): A grade option that allows you to take a class without it affecting your GPA.

NONACADEMIC WORLD: The professional realm outside of universities and research institutions, including government, nonprofits, and private companies.

PELL GRANT: A federal grant awarded to undergraduate students who demonstrate financial need.

PERSONAL STATEMENT: Often interchangeable with "Statement of Purpose." This is an essay that is a crucial part of a graduate school application, in which an applicant can explain why they are a good fit for a program. This term is often used in conjunction with *Professional Statement* or *Research Statement*.

PHD (DOCTOR OF PHILOSOPHY): A degree focused on research and academic scholarship that prepares students to be experts in a specific field.

PHD-GRANTING UNIVERSITIES: Universities that have the authority to grant doctoral degrees.

PREDATORY COLLEGES: Institutions, often private, that are more focused on collecting tuition and financial aid money than on providing a high-quality education or offering support to students.

PRIVATE INSTITUTION/UNIVERSITY: A college or university that is not funded or operated by a state government.

PROFESSIONAL STATEMENT: Often PhD programs will ask for both a "Personal Statement" and a "Professional Statement" or a "Research Statement." If they ask for both, the "Professional Statement" often is a space for you to describe the academic and other preparation and qualifications that will make you a good fit for the program you are applying to.

PUBLIC INSTITUTION/UNIVERSITY: A college or university that is funded and operated by a state government, often with lower tuition costs.

RESEARCH PROPOSAL: A plan outlining a research project, including goals, methods, and expected outcomes, which may be required with some academic applications.

RESEARCH STATEMENT: PhD programs will sometimes ask for a "Research Statement" alongside a "Personal Statement" or "Statement of Purpose." Essentially, the programs are asking you to describe the areas you want to research, the methods you are interested in using, and why you are interested in these areas. You will also want to talk about which professors in the department would be a good fit for you to work with on this topic.

RÉSUMÉ: A document similar to a CV but typically shorter and more focused on employment history and skills, commonly used for job applications outside of academic contexts.

ROLLING ADMISSIONS: An admissions process in which the program reviews applications and makes decisions as they are received, rather than waiting for a specific deadline.

STATEMENT OF PURPOSE: An essay that is a crucial part of a graduate school application, in which an applicant can explain why they are a good fit for a program. This term is often used interchangeably with *Personal Statement*, or in conjunction with *Professional Statement* or *Research Statement*.

SYLLABUS: A document provided by an instructor for a course that outlines the topics to be covered, assignments, grading policies, and other expectations.

TEAM MEMBERS (MENTORSHIP TEAM): Advisors, mentors, or peers who can offer guidance on the application process.

TENURE: A long-term employment status for professors who have passed a probationary period and have been granted a permanent position with job protections.

TENURE-TRACK PROFESSOR: A full-time, salaried professor who is on a probationary period with the potential to earn tenure.

TERMINAL MASTER'S DEGREE: A master's degree that is the highest degree offered in a particular program at a specific university and is not structured to lead into a PhD.

TEST PREP BOOKS: Books designed to help students prepare for standardized tests.

TRANSCRIPTS: A record of your academic history, including classes and grades, which you will need to submit to universities during the application process.

TRANSLATING SKILLS: The act of explaining your academic skills and experiences in a way that is relevant and understandable to people outside of your specific academic field.

TRAUMA-INFORMED CARE: An approach that recognizes the impact of past trauma on current stressors to create safe and supportive environments.

UPPER-DIVISION CLASSES: Courses typically taken in the third and fourth years of college that are relatively specialized and advanced.

VISITING ASSISTANT PROFESSOR (VAP): A temporary, full-time teaching position at a university, often lasting one or two years, which is not a permanent position.

WRITING SAMPLE: A piece of academic or professional writing that showcases your ability to communicate ideas clearly, often required for applications.

Index

Founded in 1893,
UNIVERSITY OF CALIFORNIA PRESS
publishes bold, progressive books and journals on topics in the arts, humanities, social sciences, and natural sciences—with a focus on social justice issues—that inspire thought and action among readers worldwide.

The UC PRESS FOUNDATION
raises funds to uphold the press's vital role as an independent, nonprofit publisher, and receives philanthropic support from a wide range of individuals and institutions—and from committed readers like you. To learn more, visit ucpress.edu/supportus.